THE ULTIMATE
BOOK OF
GOLF TRIVIA

Merry Christmas
Dad !
xo Court

2020

THE ULTIMATE BOOK OF GOLF TRIVIA

600 QUESTIONS AND ANSWERS

RYAN HANNABLE

Foreword by Gary Player
Afterword by Rob Oppenheim

SPORTS PUBLISHING

Sports Publishing books may be purchased in bulk at special discounts for sales promotion, corporate gifts, fund-raising, or educational purposes. Special editions can also be created to specifications. For details, contact the Special Sales Department, Sports Publishing, 307 West 36th Street, 11th Floor, New York, NY 10018 or sportspubbooks@skyhorsepublishing.com.

Sports Publishing® is a registered trademark of Skyhorse Publishing, Inc.®, a Delaware corporation.

Visit our website at www.sportspubbooks.com.

10 9 8 7 6 5 4 3 2 1

Library of Congress Cataloging-in-Publication Data

Names: Hannable, Ryan, author.
Title: The ultimate book of golf trivia : 600 questions and answers /
    Ryan Hannable ; foreword by Gary Player ; afterword by Rob Oppenheim.
Description: New York, NY : Skyhorse Publishing, 2020.
Identifiers: LCCN 2019057765 (print) | LCCN 2019057766 (ebook) | ISBN
    9781510755550 (paperback) | ISBN 9781510758926 (ebook)
Subjects: LCSH: Golf--Miscellanea.
Classification: LCC GV967 .H34 2020 (print) | LCC GV967 (ebook) | DDC
    796.352--dc23
LC record available at https://lccn.loc.gov/2019057765
LC ebook record available at https://lccn.loc.gov/2019057766

Cover design by Mona Lin
Cover photo credit Getty Images

Print ISBN: 978-1-5107-5555-0
Ebook ISBN: 978-1-5107-5892-6

Printed in the United States of America

Contents

Foreword

November 2019

I have been fortunate enough to be involved in professional golf since 1953 and it has allowed me to receive a global education traveling the world. Rest is rust, and even after my prime, I stayed involved by competing on the Senior Tour, designing courses, and hosting philanthropic charity events for children's education. The sport truly brings out the best in people and some very valuable life lessons can be taken from such a wonderful game.

Some of my accomplishments including winning 165 tournaments on six continents over seven decades, and the career Grand Slam on the Regular Tour and Senior Tour, are featured in the following pages. Also included are some of the great players and moments that followed me as well. My favorite tournaments are all featured prominently, including The Open Championship, which I won three times in three different decades, and also The Masters, which I have been lucky enough to compete in 52 times and win three times as well. It's also been a tremendous honor to return the last several years to be part of the Honorary Starter ceremony at Augusta National.

I was also extremely fortunate to serve as captain of the International team in the Presidents Cup three times, including 2003 in my home nation of South Africa. Team events in golf are exciting and after captaining the South African Olympic team at the 2016 Summer Games, I am pleased golf has a place on sport's biggest stage. I still avidly follow the game, and am so impressed with the level of play and competitiveness around the world each and every week.

The game of golf is in a great place moving forward with some tremendous stars, who are not only exceptional on the course, but also terrific people. But we must continue to innovate to make golf fun and enjoyable for all ages and skill levels. Always remember that amateurs are the game's lifeblood.

I do hope you enjoy this book as much as I enjoy playing this great game for so many years that will always be such a major part of my life.

Best wishes,

Gary Player

Gary Player

I. 1970s AND EARLIER

QUESTIONS

Golf has been around for a long time—since the 15th century in Scotland to be exact. The first 18-hole round was created at the Old Course at St. Andrews in 1764 and things have gotten bigger and bigger since.

While there were a number of big names in the earlier years, the sport really became popular in the 1970s, led by Arnold Palmer, Gary Player, and Jack Nicklaus. Without these three players, it's hard to imagine where the sport would be today.

"Golf is deceptively simple and endlessly complicated; it satisfies the soul and frustrates the intellect. It is at the same time rewarding and maddening—and it is without a doubt the greatest game mankind has ever invented."

–Arnold Palmer

"I never went into a tournament or round of golf thinking I had to beat a certain player. I had to beat the golf course. If I prepared myself for a major, went in focused, and then beat the golf course, the rest took care of itself."

–Jack Nicklaus

Answers for this section are on pages 9–11.

RED TEES

1. What was Arnold Palmer's nickname?
   A. Golden boy
   B. The King
   C. Iced Tea
   D. AP

2. Which major was last to be founded?
   A. British Open
   B. PGA Championship
   C. Masters
   D. U.S. Open

3. What were Arnold Palmer's fans referred to as?
   A. Arnie's Den
   B. Arnie's Army
   C. AP's Crew
   D. Palmer's Row

4. Which of the following was not a nickname of Gary Player's?
   A. The Black Knight
   B. The International Ambassador of Golf
   C. The Big Easy
   D. Mr. Fitness

5. Which golfer was not part of "The Big Three" in the 1950s–1970s?
   A. Gary Player
   B. Sam Snead
   C. Jack Nicklaus
   D. Arnold Palmer

6. What two drinks are combined for what is known as an "Arnold Palmer?"
   A. Lemonade and iced tea
   B. Coke and rum
   C. Lemonade and ginger ale
   D. Sprite and iced tea

WHITE TEES

7. How many majors did Arnold Palmer win?
   A. 5
   B. 7
   C. 10
   D. 12

8. True/False: Bob Charles was the first left-handed golfer to win a major.

9. Who is famous for hitting "the shot heard 'round the world?"
   A. Arnold Palmer
   B. Walter Hagan
   C. Gene Sarazen
   D. Gary Player

10. True/False: Ben Hogan had more PGA Tour wins than Arnold Palmer.

11. Sam Snead won every major except for one. Which was it?
    A. Masters
    B. PGA Championship
    C. U.S. Open
    D. British Open

12. True/False: Sam Snead won 82 tournaments, but never won more than one major in the same year.

13. True/False: Arnold Palmer won more majors than Gary Player.

14. Which major did Arnold Palmer fail to win?
    A. Masters
    B. U.S. Open
    C. PGA Championship
    D. He won all of them

15. How old was Gary Player when he completed the Grand Slam (1965)?
    A. 29
    B. 35
    C. 40
    D. 43

16. Which modern club did Gene Sarazen claim to invent?
    A. Driver
    B. Sand wedge
    C. Hybrid
    D. 5-wood

17. True/False: Gene Sarazen won the career Grand Slam.

18. How many majors did Walter Hagen win?
    A. 0
    B. 4
    C. 8
    D. 11

19. In what year was the first U.S. Open nationally televised?
    A. 1945
    B. 1950
    C. 1954
    D. 1965

20. Which was not an official event on the PGA Tour in 1975?
A. Danny Thomas Memphis Classic
B. First NBC New Orleans Open
C. Toyota Classic
D. Hawaiian Open

BLACK TEES

21. Which golfer currently has a caddie scholarship named after him?
A. Henry Vardon
B. Johnny McDermott
C. Bobby Jones
D. Francis Ouimet

22. Which Argentinian won the 1967 British Open?
A. Carlos Franco
B. Eduardo Romero
C. Roberto Di Vicenzo
D. Vincente Fernandez

23. Which player won the U.S. Open, U.S. Amateur, the British Open, and the British Amateur in the same year (1930)?
A. Francis Ouimet
B. Bobby Jones
C. Ben Hogan
D. Sam Snead

24. Who won three of the four majors in 1953?
A. Walter Hagen
B. Ben Hogan
C. Gene Sarazen
D. Gary Player

25. In 1945, how many consecutive tournaments did Bryon Nelson win?

A. 5

B. 8

C. 9

D. 11

26. Which star golfer almost died in a car accident?

A. Ben Hogan

B. Walter Hagen

C. Sam Snead

D. Bobby Jones

27. Following the near fatal crash in 1949, how many more majors did the same star golfer go on to win?

A. 0

B. 2

C. 4

D. 6

28. Arnold Palmer lost the 1966 U.S. Open in a playoff to a player who shot 32 over the final nine holes to force the extra holes. Who was that player?

A. Gary Player

B. Billy Casper

C. Bob Charles

D. Gene Sarazen

29. In what year did Arnold Palmer eclipse the $1 million career earnings mark?

A. 1960

B. 1964

C. 1968

D. 1972

30. Who won the most PGA Tour tournaments in 1978?
   A. Arnold Palmer
   B. Gary Player
   C. Jack Nicklaus
   D. Tom Watson

I. 1970s AND EARLIER

ANSWERS

RED TEES

1. B – The King. Palmer was one of golf's first major superstars and passed away in September 2016.

2. C – Masters. The Masters was not founded until 1934.

3. B – Arnie's Army. Palmer had a tremendous following at almost every tournament he played in.

4. C – The Big Easy. Player had a number of nicknames and was golf's first major international superstar.

5. B – Sam Snead. The prime of Snead's career came in the 1940s and 1950s.

6. A – Lemonade and iced tea. This drink is very popular, even outside of golf.

WHITE TEES

7. B – 7. Palmer won seven majors, including four Masters.

8. True. Charles won the British Open in 1963.

9. C – Gene Sarazen. This was at the 1935 Masters when Sarazen made a double-eagle on the par-5 fifteenth hole. He holed a 4-wood from 235 yards away.

10. True. Hogan had 64 to Palmer's 62.

11. C – U.S. Open. Snead did finish second four times, though.

12. False. Snead won the Masters and PGA Championship in 1949.

13. False. Player won nine, while Palmer won seven.

14. C – PGA Championship. Palmer did finish second three times, though.

15. A – 29. Player is one of five players to complete the career Grand Slam.

16. B – Sand wedge. Sarazen is credited with the 1935 invention.

17. True. Sarazen won the PGA Championship three times, the U.S. Open twice, as well as the Masters and British Open once each.

18. D – 11. Hagen won 11 majors, but failed to win the Masters with his best finish being T-11.

19. C – 1954. While this was the year the event was first televised, all four rounds weren't televised until 1965.

20. C – Toyota Classic. This was never a PGA Tour event. The Honda Classic is an official event now, but not the Toyota Classic.

BLACK TEES

21. D – Francis Ouimet. Ouimet is frequently referred to as the "father of amateur golf."

22. C – Roberto Di Vicenzo. This was his only major title.

23. B – Bobby Jones. Jones became the first player since John Ball in 1890 to win both the British Amateur and British Open in the same year.

24. B – Ben Hogan. Hogan failed to win the PGA Championship, as that tournament was won by Chick Harbert.

25. D – 11. In all, Nelson won 18 of 35 PGA tournaments that year.

26. A – Ben Hogan. Hogan won 63 professional tournaments despite the interruption of his career by World War II and the near-fatal car accident. He won the 1950 U.S. Open just eleven months after the February 1949 crash.

27. D – 6. Hogan won the U.S. Open three times, the Masters twice, and the British Open once following the crash, in which he suffered multiple injuries, including a double fracture of the pelvis, fractured collar bone, and a left ankle fracture.

28. B – Billy Casper. Of the 15 sub-par rounds posted in the tournament, three belonged to Casper.

29. C – 1968. Palmer won $3.6 million in prize money during his 52 years on the PGA Tour and Champions Tour, but through appearances, endorsements, etc. his estimated career earnings is said to be in the $875 million range.

30. D – Tom Watson. Watson won five tournaments, and there were seven first-time winners.

II. 1980s

QUESTIONS

Following Arnold Palmer, Gary Player, and Jack Nicklaus dominating the 1970s, the 1980s were a time for some new players to take over. There wasn't one particular player to dominate, as a number of different players had years where they were stars of the game.

Notable players to emerge during this time included Greg Norman, Curtis Strange, Tom Watson, Seve Ballesteros and Lee Trevino. Nicklaus didn't completely go away during this time, either. Three of his 15 majors came in the 80s.

"I always wanted to be the best I could be at whatever I did. I didn't want to be the No. 1 golfer in the world. I just wanted to be as good as I could be. I work hard, I push myself hard, and I probably even expect too much of myself."

–Greg Norman

"I didn't learn how to swing a golf club until late in my career. And even though I won all those tournaments, I still struggled with consistency, and I relied on my strengths, which were hitting the ball long and high, and I could chip and putt with the best of 'em."

–Tom Watson

Answers for this section are on pages 19–22.

RED TEES

1. What was Jack Nicklaus's nickname?
   A. The Golden Bear
   B. The Lion
   C. Gentle Giant
   D. The Animal

2. Which golfer won the British Open three out of four years from 1980–83?
   A. Tom Watson
   B. Jack Nicklaus
   C. Seve Ballesteros
   D. Hale Irvin

3. Which golfer is nicknamed "The Walrus"?
   A. Bernhard Langer
   B. Craig Stadler
   C. Hal Sutton
   D. Bill Rogers

4. True/False: The World Series of Golf was an official PGA Tour event in 1980.

WHITE TEES

5. Which major was Jack Nicklaus's 18th and final one?
   A. Masters
   B. U.S. Open
   C. PGA Championship
   D. British Open

6. Which golfer was married to tennis star Chris Evert for less than 2 years?
A. Nick Faldo
B. Tom Kite
C. Jack Nicklaus
D. Greg Norman

7. True/False: Jack Nicklaus's first professional win was the U.S. Open.

8. True/False: Fuzzy Zoeller won the Masters in his first appearance at the event.

9. Which player won back-to-back U.S. Opens in 1988–89?
A. Curtis Strange
B. Tom Watson
C. Hale Irvin
D. Larry Nelson

10. True/False: In 1986, Greg Norman held the lead in every major after 54 holes, but only won one of them.

11. Tom Watson won eight major titles throughout his career, but never at which major tournament?
A. Masters
B. U.S. Open
C. British Open
D. PGA Championship

12. What is Sandy Lyle's nationality?
A. American
B. Scottish
C. German
D. Canadian

13. True/False: Raymond Floyd was one major shy of the career Grand Slam, failing to win the Masters.

14. True/False: Tom Kite won 11 times in the 1980s, but none of the titles were majors.

15. True/False: Greg Norman was never the world's No. 1 player.

16. How many majors did Johnny Miller win in the 1980s?
A. 0
B. 1
C. 2
D. 4

17. How many majors did Hal Sutton win?
A. 1
B. 3
C. 4
D. 5

BLACK TEES

18. What is the only Grand Slam tournament Lee Trevino did not win?
A. Masters
B. PGA Championship
C. British Open
D. U.S. Open

19. How old was Seve Ballesteros when he won his first Masters in 1980?
A. 23
B. 25
C. 30
D. 35

20. How many runner-up finishes in majors did Ben Crenshaw have before winning the 1984 Masters?

A. 2

B. 4

C. 5

D. 6

21. Who had the most PGA Tour wins in the 1986 season with four?

A. Jack Nicklaus

B. Tom Watson

C. Bob Tway

D. Greg Norman

22. In 1980, which golfer won the most tournaments on the PGA Tour (7) and also the most money?

A. Curtis Strange

B. Lee Trevino

C. Tom Watson

D. Craig Stadler

23. Who was the PGA Tour's leading money winner in both 1981 and 1989?

A. Tom Watson

B. Tom Kite

C. Lee Trevino

D. Hale Irvin

24. Which 10-time PGA Tour winner, including three majors, didn't take up golf until he was 21 because he served in U.S. Infantry in Vietnam?

A. Larry Nelson

B. Bill Rogers

C. Hal Sutton

D. Curtis Strange

25. How many years did Curtis Strange win the PGA Tour money title in the 1980s?
A. 0
B. 1
C. 3
D. 5

26. True/False: Lee Trevino's final PGA Tour win was a major in the 1984 season.

27. Who was the 1989 PGA Tour's Player of the Year?
A. Tom Kite
B. Tom Watson
C. Lee Trevino
D. Curtis Strange

28. Tom Watson and which player led the PGA Tour in wins during the 1984 season with three?
A. Denis Watson
B. Gary Koch
C. Curtis Strange
D. Fuzzy Zoeller

29. True/False: Bob Tway once made a 12 on the famous seventeeth hole at TPC Sawgrass.

30. Tom Watson won five out of six PGA Tour Player of the Year awards from 1977–82. Who won it in 1981?
A. Bill Rogers
B. Jack Nicklaus
C. Lanny Watkins
D. Bob Tway

II. 1980s

ANSWERS

RED TEES

1. A – The Golden Bear. The nickname came about in 1961 when Nicklaus and his wife Barbara went to Australia and there was a newspaper headline that read, "Golden Bear from U.S. to Arrive Today." Nicklaus's high school's nickname was the golden bears, so it only seemed right to adopt the nickname since he was looking for a personal logo at the time.

2. A – Tom Watson. Watson also won the Masters and U.S. Open during this time.

3. B – Craig Stadler. Stadler has 13 career PGA Tour wins, including the 1982 Masters. The nickname comes from his trademark facial hair.

4. True. Tom Watson won the tournament, which was his 25th on Tour.

WHITE TEES

5. A – Masters. Nicklaus won the 1986 Masters by one stroke over Tom Kite and Greg Norman.

6. D – Greg Norman. It was reported the marriage ended because of "huge egos" for the pair. The two separated after 15 months following being married in June of 2008. It was Norman's second marriage, while it was Evert's third.

7. True. Nicklaus won the 1962 U.S. Open in a playoff over Arnold Palmer. The majority of his career wins took place in the 1980s.

8. True. The only two other golfers to have won the Masters in their debuts before him were Horton Smith and Gene Sarazen.

9. A – Curtis Strange. In 1988 he beat Nick Faldo in a playoff, and then the following year beat Chip Beck, Mark McCumber, and Ian Woosman by one stroke.

10. True. Despite leading every major after 54 holes, the only major victory Norman claimed that year was the British Open.

11. D – PGA Championship. Watson's best finish in the tournament was T-2 in 1978.

12. B – Scotland. Lyle was born in England, but now lives in Scotland. He's most known for winning the 1985 British Open and 1988 Masters.

13. False. Floyd won the Masters in 1976. He has won every major except the British Open.

14. True. Kite's only major was the U.S. Open, which came in 1992.

15. False. Norman spent 331 weeks as the world's No. 1 player beginning in 1986.

16. A – 0. Miller's two majors came in 1973 and 1976.

17. A – 1. Sutton won the 1983 PGA Championship.

BLACK TEES

18. A – Masters. Trevino won every other major twice, but does not have a Masters title. His best finish is a tie for 10th.

19. A – 23. At the time, Ballesteros was the youngest player ever to win the Masters. That record was later broken by Tiger Woods.

20. C – 5. Crenshaw was even the runner-up in the 1983 Masters before he finally was able to claim the first of his two majors, both coming at Augusta.

21. C – Bob Tway. While Tway won the most tournaments that year, Greg Norman was the leading money winner.

22. C – Tom Watson. Watson's seven wins included one major—the British Open.

23. B – Tom Kite. Kite only won one tournament in 1981, but three in 1989.

24. A – Larry Nelson. His three majors include two PGA Championships and a British Open.

25. C – 3. Strange was the PGA Tour money winner in 1985, 1987 and 1988. Overall, he won 17 PGA Tour events.

26. True. Trevino won the 1984 PGA Championship by four strokes over Gary Player and Lanny Watkins.

27. A – Tom Kite. Kite finished that year with three wins and was also the Tour's leading money winner.

28. A – Denis Watson. All of his wins came in August and September, as he won the Buick Open, the NEC World Series of Golf, and the Panasonic Las Vegas Invitational.

29. True. It was the third round of the 2005 PLAYERS. He hit four balls into the water surrounding the island green.

30. A – Bill Rogers. Rogers won four tournaments that year and was fifth on the money list. One of his wins was at the British Open.

III. 1990s

QUESTIONS

The 1990s might most be remembered for the Tiger Woods era beginning. Woods made his first PGA Tour start in 1996 and officially joined the Tour in the same year at the age of 20.

While Woods's name dominates the headlines from these years, there were still some other big names and unique stories. One of the most unique was John Daly's two majors, but Nick Price, Payne Stewart, and Mark O'Meara were also very good players.

Overall, these years were without a true, true star and Woods's emergence was just what the sport needed.

"If somebody asks for my opinion, I tell them my opinion, whether it's what they want to hear or not."

–Payne Stewart

"I hit the ball as hard as I can. If I can find it, I hit it again."

–John Daly

Answers for this section are on pages 29–32.

RED TEES

1. Who is nicknamed "The Big Easy" and won two U.S. Opens in the 1990s?
A. Payne Stewart
B. Ernie Els
C. Tom Kite
D. Hale Irwin

2. Which of the following is not a nickname for John Daly?
A. Wild Thing
B. Big D
C. Long John
D. The Lion

3. Which country is Jesper Parnevik from?
A. England
B. Spain
C. Australia
D. Sweden

4. Who is the father of current PGA Tour player Bill Haas, who won 33 professional events, including nine on the PGA Tour?
A. Jay Haas
B. Tim Haas
C. Phil Haas
D. Paul Haas

WHITE TEES

5. Where did Payne Stewart win his third and final major?
A. Bethpage Black
B. Pebble Beach
C. Pinehurst No. 2
D. The Country Club

6. True/False: After winning back-to-back U.S. Opens in 1988–89, Curtis Strange missed the cut in 1990.

7. Which South African won back-to-back majors in 1994?
A. Ernie Els
B. Retief Goosen
C. Vijay Singh
D. Nick Price

8. True/False: 1994 is the only year an American golfer did not win a major when all four were held.

9. Which was not an official PGA Tour tournament in 1994?
A. Bellsouth Classic
B. Nestle Invitational
C. Kmart Greater Greensboro Open
D. Honda Challenge

10. Tiger Woods was the leading money winner in 1997. Who was second?
A. Davis Love III
B. David Duval
C. Tom Lehman
D. Nick Price

11. True/False: David Duval won more tournaments in 1998 than Tiger Woods.

12. In 1998, which tournament was shortened to 54 holes with the first 36 holes being in February and the final 18 in August?
A. Phoenix Open
B. Buick Open
C. AT&T Pebble Beach Pro-Am
D. Nissan Open

13. True/False: In 1991, no player won more than two tournaments.

14. Which country is Steve Elkington from?
   A. Canada
   B. Australia
   C. United States
   D. Germany

15. True/False: José María Olazábal won the British Open twice in the 1990s.

16. How many majors did Justin Leonard win?
   A. 1
   B. 4
   C. 5
   D. 6

17. True/False: Brad Faxon has never won a major.

18. Which country is Carlos Franco from?
   A. Spain
   B. Germany
   C. Paraguay
   D. Mexico

19. True/False: Nick Price was never the No. 1 ranked player in the world.

BLACK TEES

20. What major was Fred Couples's first and only?
   A. PGA Championship
   B. Masters
   C. U.S. Open
   D. British Open

21. The 1990s saw a few players win their first and only major. Who was not one of them?
   A. Mark Brooks
   B. Tom Kite
   C. Lee Janzen
   D. Fred Couples

22. Ian Woosnam won his only major in 1991. Which one was it?
   A. Masters
   B. U.S. Open
   C. PGA Championship
   D. British Open

23. Who was the 1999 PGA Tour Rookie of the Year?
   A. Rich Beem
   B. Carlos Franco
   C. Notah Begay III
   D. Jeff Maggert

24. Who won the most PGA Tour tournaments in 1990?
   A. Wayne Levi
   B. Mark O'Meara
   C. Payne Stewart
   D. Nick Faldo

25. Who won the 1991 PGA Tour Player of the Year?
   A. Corey Pavin
   B. Mark O'Meara
   C. Tom Kite
   D. Ernie Els

26. Which golfer won The Skins Game (an event to which four players were invited to play each hole match play style with the winner of each hole earning a "skin") three straight years from 1991–93?
    A. Davis Love III
    B. Payne Stewart
    C. Tom Watson
    D. Fred Couples

27. What happened in 1999 that allowed caddies to temporarily wear shorts?
    A. Too many caddies complained
    B. A caddie collapsed during competition
    C. A rule change was passed by the Tour
    D. Caddies have never been allowed to wear shorts

28. What year did Ben Crenshaw win his final PGA Tour event?
    A. 1990
    B. 1992
    C. 1995
    D. 1999

29. Which year did Lee Westwood claim his first PGA Tour win?
    A. 1990
    B. 1992
    C. 1994
    D. 1998

30. Which tournament did Jim Furyk win three times in the late 1990s?
    A. Las Vegas Invitational
    B. Canadian Open
    C. Genesis Open
    D. Buick Invitational

III. 1990s

ANSWERS

RED TEES

1. B – Ernie Els. Overall, Els has won 19 times on the PGA Tour and another 28 on the European Tour. In addition to the two U.S. Opens, he also won the British Open in 2002 and 2012.

2. B – Big D. Daly won five total times on the PGA Tour and is most known for his PGA Championship in 1991 and British Open in 1995.

3. D – Sweden. Despite no majors, Parnevik won five times on the PGA Tour and another four on the European Tour.

4. A – Jay Haas. Golf runs in the family, as Bill is a nephew of the 1968 Masters winner Bob Goalby. Bill's brother Jerry Haas and brother-in-law Dillard Pruitt both played on the PGA Tour, as well.

WHITE TEES

5. C – Pinehurst No. 2. Stewart's final major was the 1999 U.S. Open where he won by one stroke over Phil Mickelson.

6. False. Strange finished T-21 in the 1990 U.S. Open.

7. D – Nick Price. Price won the British Open and PGA Championship. He had six total wins in 1994.

8. True. José María Olazábel, Ernie Els, and Nick Price (twice) were the major winners in 1994.

9. D – Honda Challenge. The Honda Challenge has never been a PGA Tour event, although the Honda Classic is an event held each spring in Florida.

10. B – David Duval. Duval won three times that year to Woods's four times.

11. True. Duval won four times, while Woods only one once.

12. C – AT&T Pebble Beach Pro-Am. Phil Mickelson won with a final score of 14-under.

13. True. In 1991, Billy Andrade, Mark Brooks, Fred Couples, Andrew Magee, Corey Pavin, Nick Price, Tom Purtzer, and Ian Woosnam all won twice, but no one won three times.

14. B – Australia. Elkington won 10 times on the PGA Tour, most notably the 1995 PGA Championship.

15. False. María Olazábal won the Masters twice in the 1990s (1994 and 1999).

16. A – 1. Leonard's lone major came in the 1997 British Open. He has finished second twice at the PGA Championship, though.

17. True. Faxon's highest finish at a major was the 1995 PGA Championship when he finished fifth.

18. C – Paraguay. Franco was the first rookie to surpass $1 million in earnings in a season and he enjoyed quite a bit of success playing around the world.

19. False. Price spent 44 weeks as the world's No. 1 player in 1994.

BLACK TEES

20. B – Masters. Couples won the 1992 Masters at 13-under, beating Raymond Floyd by two strokes.

21. C – Lee Janzen. Janzen won the 1993 and 1998 U.S. Opens, so he won two majors in the 1990s.

22. A – Masters. Woosnam won the 1991 Masters by one stroke over José María Olazábal.

23. B – Carlos Franco. He won twice that year—Compaq Classic of New Orleans and Greater Milwaukee Open.

24. A – Wayne Levi. He won four times and finished second on the money list behind Greg Norman.

25. A – Corey Pavin. Pavin was the leading money winner for that year and finished second in scoring average, decimal points behind Fred Couples.

26. B – Payne Stewart. Fred Couples was runner-up in the event twice, while John Daly was runner-up the other time.

27. B – A caddie collapsed during competition. Garland Dempsey collapsed due to heat at the Western Open in early July. This incident allowed caddies to wear shorts all the time, which is still a rule today.

28. C – 1995. It was the Masters where he defeated Davis Love III by one stroke. That was his second Masters victory.

29. D – 1998. It was at the Freeport-McDermott Classic. Despite a number of wins worldwide, Westwood has only won twice on the PGA Tour.

30. A – Las Vegas Invitational. Furyk won the tournament in 1995 (first career win), 1998, and 1999. All the victories were by one stroke.

IV. 2000s

QUESTIONS

This era was dominated by Tiger Woods, but he was also challenged multiple times by David Duval and Vijay Singh, as well as Phil Mickelson.

Given the run Woods went on over these years, the sport became as popular as it had ever been with a record number of people tuning into tournaments every week. It also saw some of the stars of today begin their careers on Tour.

"I didn't do anything spectacular when I won the Open in 2001. I hit the ball good, not great. I putted good, not great, but I think I missed maybe two putts inside eight feet all week."

–David Duval

"I want to play golf, practice, and not do much else. I don't drink, I don't smoke, and I hate going places where you have to yell at someone who is about a foot away from you."

–Vijay Singh

Answers for this section are on pages 39–42.

RED TEES

1. Who is nicknamed "The Goose" and won two U.S. Opens in the 2000s?
   A. Ernie Els
   B. Retief Goosen
   C. John Daly
   D. Curtis Strange

2. Where is Vijay Singh from?
   A. South Africa
   B. New Zealand
   C. Philippines
   D. Fiji

3. Which country is Geoff Ogilvy from?
   A. Australia
   B. New Zealand
   C. Canada
   D. United States

4. What state was Zach Johnson born in?
   A. Florida
   B. Iowa
   C. California
   D. Texas

5. What made the Showdown at Sherwood, Battle at Bighorn, and Battle at the Bridges so special?
   A. The top two money winners faced each other
   B. The event was televised in primetime on Monday nights
   C. Tiger Woods played from tips, while other golfers played forward tees
   D. The event had a special scoring format, as players got points for hard shots

6. True/False: K.J. Choi has never won a major.

WHITE TEES

7. How many majors has Vijay Singh won?
   A. 1
   B. 3
   C. 6
   D. 7

8. Who replaced Ken Venturi as the lead analyst on CBS in 2003?
   A. Nick Faldo
   B. Ian Woosnam
   C. Lanny Wadkins
   D. Judy Rankin

9. Who was the PGA Tour money winner in 2003?
   A. Vijay Singh
   B. Phil Mickelson
   C. Tiger Woods
   D. Mike Weir

10. How many majors has Davis Love III won?
   A. 1
   B. 3
   C. 5
   D. 7

11. Which golfer is nicknamed Spider-Man?
   A. Sergio Garcia
   B. Camilo Villegas
   C. Anthony Kim
   D. Adam Scott

12. Who was the PGA Tour Player of the Year in 2008?
    A. Tiger Woods
    B. Vijay Singh
    C. Stewart Cink
    D. Padraig Harrington

13. Which country is Stephen Ames from?
    A. Canada
    B. United States
    C. Australia
    D. New Zealand

14. Which state is Steve Stricker from?
    A. Florida
    B. Texas
    C. Wisconsin
    D. California

15. Who was the first Korean to win on the PGA Tour?
    A. K.J. Choi
    B. Charlie Wi
    C. Si-woo Kim
    D. Kevin Na

16. True/False: Vijay Singh was a three-time PGA Tour money winner in the 2000s.

17. Who did Tiger Woods face and lose to at the 2000 Battle at Bighorn?
    A. Sergio Garcia
    B. David Duval
    C. Vijay Singh
    D. Phil Mickelson

18. True/False: Vijay Singh was never the world No. 1 player.

19. True/False: David Duval has won only one major.

20. True/False: Padraig Harrington won back-to-back majors in 2008.

21. Which of the following was not an official PGA Tour event in 2001?
A. MasterCard Colonial
B. Kemper Insurance Open
C. Advil Western Open
D. M&M Classic

22. True/False: David Duval spent 15 weeks as the world's No. 1 player.

23. True/False: Davis Love III is not in the World Golf Hall of Fame.

BLACK TEES

24. Which player lost majors in playoffs in back-to-back years (2004 PGA Championship and 2005 Masters)?
A. Chris DiMarco
B. Mike Weir
C. Lee Westwood
D. K.J. Choi

25. In 2007, who won the Wyndham Championship and then went on to win the PGA Tour Rookie of the Year?
A. K.J. Choi
B. Brandt Snedeker
C. Stephen Ames
D. Chad Campbell

26. Who is the oldest player to win the PLAYERS at age 48?
A. Craig Perks
B. Hal Sutton
C. Fred Funk
D. Tim Clark

27. Chris DiMarco finished second in three of the four majors. Which one hasn't he finished second in?
A. Masters
B. U.S. Open
C. PGA Championship
D. British Open

28. In addition to the AT&T Pebble Beach Pro-Am, which event was another pro-am event in the 2000s?
A. Ford Championship at Doral
B. Bob Hope Chrysler Classic
C. Cialis Western Open
D. Booz Allen Classic

29. In 2009, which tournament was outright cancelled due to rain?
A. AT&T Pebble Beach Pro-Am
B. Honda Classic
C. Viking Classic
D. RBC Canadian Open

30. Which player did not win a FedEx Cup event in 2009?
A. Tiger Woods
B. Steve Stricker
C. Heath Slocum
D. Matt Kuchar

IV. 2000

ANSWERS

RED TEES

1. B – Retief Goosen. The two U.S. Opens were his only two majors, but he always showed well, seemingly always being at the top of the leaderboard on the weekend.

2. D – Fiji. Singh won 34 times on the PGA Tour and another 13 times on the European Tour.

3. A – Australia. He is most known for his 2006 U.S. Open and his highest world ranking was No. 3.

4. B – Iowa. Johnson has two major titles to his name—the 2007 Masters and the 2015 British Open.

5. B – The event was televised in primetime on Monday nights. It was very popular in the 2000s, which included some courses having lights installed for the final few holes.

6. True. The Korean does have three top-10s in majors, though. His best finish was third at the 2004 Masters.

WHITE TEES

7. B – 3. He won the PGA Championship in 1998 and 2004 and the Masters in 2000.

8. C – Lanny Watkins. He served in this role for four years until he was replaced by Nick Faldo after the 2006 season.

9. A – Vijay Singh. Singh was the leading money winner in 2003 despite Tiger Woods winning one more tournament than he did.

10. A – 1. He won the 1997 PGA Championship when he ran away from the field and won by five strokes at 11-under par.

11. B – Camilo Villegas. The Columbian was very popular in the 2000s, as he won four times on the PGA Tour.

12. D – Padraig Harrington. After winning the season's final two majors, he was pretty much a lock for the Player of the Year award.

13. A – Canada. Ames lives in Canada, but was born in Trinidad and Tobago. He has four career PGA Tour wins and two European Tour wins.

14. C – Wisconsin. The Wisconsin native is one of the best players never to win a major. His best career finish was second at the 1998 PGA Championship.

15. A – K.J. Choi. In 2002, Choi won the Compaq Classic of New Orleans by four strokes.

16. True. The Fijian was the leading money winner in 2003, 2004, and 2008. He was also the PGA Tour's Player of the Year in 2004.

17. A – Sergio Garcia. This was highly anticipated following Garcia and Woods's battle at the PGA Championship the year before. Garcia won 1-up.

18. False. Singh was the world's No. 1 player for 32 weeks beginning in September of 2004.

19. True. Despite winning 13 PGA Tour events and going toe-to-toe with Tiger Woods at a number of them, Duval only has one major to his name—the 2001 British Open.

20. True. Harrington also won the PGA Tour's Player of the Year that year.

21. D – M&M Classic. This has never been a PGA Tour event.

22. True. This took place in 1999 when Duval spent 15 weeks as the world's No. 1 player.

23. False. Love III was inducted in 2017. He's won 21 times on the PGA Tour.

BLACK TEES

24. A – Chris DiMarco. He has never won a major, which makes those playoff defeats even more crushing.

25. B – Brandt Snedeker. The Tennessee native also won the event 11 years later when he claimed the Wyndham Championship in 2018.

26. C – Fred Funk. He won the event in 2005 by one stroke over three players—Luke Donald, Scott Verplank, and Tom Lehman.

27. B – U.S. Open. His best finish at this major was T-9 in 2004.

28. B – Bob Hope Chrysler Classic. It is now the Desert Classic presented by Workday.

29. C – Viking Classic. Madison, Mississippi, received over 20 inches of rain in the six weeks before the tournament, which made the course unplayable.

30. D – Matt Kuchar. Woods won the BMW Championship, Stricker won the Deutsche Bank Championship, and Slocum won The Barclays.

V. PRESENT DAY

QUESTIONS

It can be said professional golf has never been as popular as it is today. The past few years have seen Tiger Woods go away then return with great authority (none bigger than his win at the 2019 Masters), but his absence allowed for a new generation of players to take over the game.

The game is littered with stars, including Rory McIlroy, Justin Thomas, Jordan Spieth, Brooks Koepka, Dustin Johnson, and more. In the post Woods dominant era, no one has been able to take over the game like he did, which is a testament to just how good the PGA Tour is now. Each week a number of different players have a chance to win, and that simply wasn't the case 10–15 years ago.

The sport is also more accessible than ever before. There's plenty of coverage on the weekends from the major networks, but also 24/7 with the Golf Channel, in addition to popular YouTube channels, podcasts, etc.

"You know I need that cockiness, the self-belief, arrogance, swagger, whatever you want to call it, I need that on the golf course to bring the best out of myself. So you know once I leave the golf course, you know that all gets left there."

–Rory McIlroy

"The game is getting younger and the game is getting better. It has to do with Tiger and Phil, largely, inspiring everybody and brought a lot more youth into the game of golf."

–Jordan Spieth

Answers for this section are on pages 53–58.

RED TEES

1. At the 2016 Summer Olympics in Rio de Janeiro, which golfer won gold in the men's individual tournament?
   A. Jordan Spieth
   B. Sergio Garcia
   C. Rory McIlroy
   D. Justin Rose

2. Justin Rose won the 2018 FedEx Cup, but who won the TOUR Championship that same week?
   A. Jordan Spieth
   B. Rory McIlroy
   C. Tiger Woods
   D. Justin Thomas

3. Which golfer is nicknamed "lefty"?
   A. Mike Weir
   B. Brian Harmon
   C. Phil Mickelson
   D. Bubba Watson

4. Who sponsors Rickie Fowler?
   A. Under Armour
   B. Adidas
   C. Nike
   D. Puma

5. What country is Adam Scott from?
   A. United States
   B. Canada
   C. Australia
   D. England

6. Which golfer is famous for having clubs that are the same length?
   A. Bryson DeChambeau
   B. Gary Woodland
   C. Adam Scott
   D. Justin Thomas

7. Which golfer is engaged to hockey great Wayne Gretzky's daughter, Paulina?
   A. Dustin Johnson
   B. Kevin Kisner
   C. Brooks Koepka
   D. Pat Perez

8. What is not something associated with J.B. Holmes?
   A. Is from Kentucky
   B. Known for hitting long ball
   C. Was a rookie in 2006 with Bubba Watson
   D. Has a runner-up finish in major

9. Phil Mickelson has won three of the four majors. Which major hasn't he won?
   A. Masters
   B. U.S. Open
   C. British Open
   D. PGA Championship

10. What is Patrick Reed's nickname?
    A. Captain America
    B. P-Reed
    C. Red, white, and blue
    D. Patty

11. True/False: Brooks Koepka has never been the world No. 1 player.

WHITE TEES

12. True/False: Hideki Matsuyama was the first Japanese player to win a PGA Tour event.

13. Which player, like Tiger Woods, typically wears red on Sundays?
    A. Patrick Reed
    B. Rory McIlroy
    C. Pat Perez
    D. Justin Thomas

14. Which golfer has reportedly had his parents removed from watching him at tournaments and has his brother-in-law as his caddie?
    A. Patrick Reed
    B. Dustin Johnson
    C. Ian Poulter
    D. Webb Simpson

15. What is Ian Poulter's nickname?
    A. The Walrus
    B. The Postman
    C. The Volcano
    D. The Lion

16. True/False: Jason Day has never been ranked No. 1 in the world.

17. Which player had an issue when he won the Mayakoba Golf Classic in Mexico in 2018 when he didn't pay a fill-in caddie the proper amount?
A. Dustin Johnson
B. Patrick Reed
C. Jordan Spieth
D. Matt Kuchar

18. There has only been one two-time winner of the FedEx Cup besides Tiger Woods. Who is it?
A. Bubba Watson
B. Justin Thomas
C. Jordan Spieth
D. Rory McIlroy

19. Where did Jordan Spieth go to college?
A. Stanford
B. University of Texas
C. UCLA
D. Oklahoma

20. True/False: Justin Thomas's first two PGA Tour wins were when he won the CIMB Classic in back-to-back years.

21. What is Xander Schauffele's given first name?
A. Alexander
B. William
C. Alex
D. Xander

22. True/False: Tiger Woods's old caddie Steve Williams has caddied for Justin Rose and Adam Scott.

23. What state is Phil Mickelson from?
   A. New York
   B. Florida
   C. California
   D. Texas

24. How many tournaments did Jordan Spieth win in 2015 when he won PGA Tour Player of the Year?
   A. 3
   B. 4
   C. 5
   D. 7

25. Who recorded a 16 on the par-4 ninth hole during the 2011 Valero Texas Open?
   A. Webb Simpson
   B. Kevin Na
   C. Bill Haas
   D. Phil Mickelson

26. Where did Jason Dufner go to college?
   A. Alabama
   B. Auburn
   C. South Carolina
   D. Tennessee

27. Who won the 2014 FedEx Cup?
   A. Rory McIlroy
   B. Bill Haas
   C. Tiger Woods
   D. Billy Horschel

28. Which player almost had a hole-in-one on the 433-yard par-4 twelfth hole during the 2018 Sentry Tournament of Champions?
A. Gary Woodland
B. Bubba Watson
C. Dustin Johnson
D. J.B. Holmes

29. Which rookie in 2019 won the 3M Open on a sponsors exemption?
A. Matthew Wolf
B. Collin Morikawa
C. Cameron Champ
D. Aaron Wise

30. True/False: Dustin Johnson has either won or finished second in all four majors.

31. True/False: In 2012, Rory McIlroy was the PGA Tour's Player of the Year, but missed out on the European Golfer of the Year despite winning the Race to Dubai.

32. True/False: Jim Furyk has not won the FedEx Cup.

33. Jimmy Walker has won one major. Which one was it?
A. Masters
B. U.S. Open
C. PGA Championship
D. British Open

34. True/False: Lee Westwood went four straight years finishing second in at least one major.

35. Which tournament was Jordan Spieth's first PGA Tour win?

A. Masters

B. John Deere Classic

C. British Open

D. Travelers Championship

36. Which year did Rory McIlroy win the final two majors—the British Open and PGA Championship?

A. Never

B. 2012

C. 2014

D. 2016

37. True/False: Bubba Watson has won two majors, both at the Masters.

38. Who was the 2016 PGA Tour Player of the Year despite Rory McIlroy winning the FedEx Cup?

A. Dustin Johnson

B. Jordan Spieth

C. Adam Scott

D. Phil Mickelson

39. What college did Rickie Fowler attend?

A. Stanford

B. Texas

C. Oklahoma State

D. UCLA

40. What is Billy Horschel's biggest accomplishment on the PGA Tour?

A. Shooting 59

B. Winning PGA Championship

C. Winning FedEx Cup

D. Recording two hole-in-ones in same round

41. What state is Justin Thomas from?
A. Texas
B. Kentucky
C. Florida
D. California

BLACK TEES

42. At what tournament did Brooks Koepka claim his first PGA Tour win?
A. U.S. Open
B. Waste Management Open
C. PGA Championship
D. Honda Classic

43. There have been three multiple winners of the WGC Match Play Event. Tiger Woods and Jason Day are two of them, who is the third?
A. Bubba Watson
B. Geoff Ogilvy
C. Matt Kuchar
D. Rory McIlroy

44. True/False: Jon Rahm's first professional win came on the PGA Tour, not the European Tour.

45. How many of Bubba Watson's wins have come in playoffs?
A. 0
B. 1
C. 2
D. 5

46. True/False: Besides the British Open, Louis Oosthuizen has never won an official PGA Tour event.

47. Which golfer's aunt is Hall of Famer Pat Bradley?
  A. Justin Thomas
  B. Bubba Watson
  C. Keegan Bradley
  D. Matt Kuchar

48. What tournament did Jim Furyk shoot a 58 at in 2016?
  A. Travelers Championship
  B. Wells Fargo Championship
  C. Genesis Open
  D. John Deere Classic

49. Who won the PGA Tour Player of the Year in 2011?
  A. Luke Donald
  B. Jim Furyk
  C. Vijay Singh
  D. Phil Mickelson

50. Who won the PGA Tour's Rookie of the Year in 2017?
  A. Justin Thomas
  B. Xander Schauffele
  C. Jon Rahm
  D. Brooks Koepka

V. PRESENT DAY

ANSWERS

RED TEES

1. D – Justin Rose. Rose won the gold medal by one stroke over Henrik Stenson with a birdie on the final hole. American Matt Kuchar won the bronze.

2. C – Tiger Woods. It was Woods's first PGA Tour win in more than five seasons. Woods won by two strokes over Billy Horschel.

3. C – Phil Mickelson. Although Mickelson plays golf left-handed, he does everything else right-handed. He learned the game by mirroring his father's right-handed swing.

4. D – Puma. Fowler is also known for wearing orange every Sunday.

5. C – Australia. Scott has 13 career PGA Tour wins to his name and was even the world's No. 1 player for 11 weeks in 2014.

6. A – Bryson DeChambeau. Not only is he famous for his clubs, he's probably most known for his slow play because of all the formulas he calculates on each shot. It's been heavily criticized on Tour.

7. A – Dustin Johnson. The two got engaged in August of 2013 and have two sons together. Johnson and Wayne Gretsky have played together in several tournaments, including the AT&T Pebble Beach Pro-Am.

8. D – Has a runner-up finish in major. While Holmes has been at the top of the leaderboard in a few majors, his best finish is a third place finish at the 2016 British Open.

9. B – U.S. Open. While Mickelson has yet to win the tournament, he has six runner-up finishes – 1999, 2002, 2004, 2006, 2009, and 2013.

10. A – Captain America. Reed earned the nickname for all his success representing the United States in team events, as well as his fiery competitiveness.

11. False. Koepka became world No. 1 for the first time in October of 2018. Winning four majors in a three-year span, it's no surprise.

WHITE TEES

12. False. In 2008, Ryuji Imada won the 2008 AT&T Classic. Matsuyama's first PGA Tour win came in 2014 when he won the Memorial Tournament.

13. A – Patrick Reed. Reed has won seven times on the PGA Tour, including the 2018 Masters. Reed says he does it in honor of Tiger Woods.

14. A – Patrick Reed. Reed has estranged from his parents Bill and Jeannette to the point where they watched him win the Masters from their home instead of at Augusta National. Reed's wife Justine also serves as his manager.

15. B – The Postman. Poulter is one of the best match play players in the entire world and has three PGA Tour wins, as well as 12 European wins to his name. The nickname comes from all the success he's had in the Ryder Cup and delivering Team Europe points.

16. False. Day became the No. 1 golfer in the world in September of 2015. The Australian has one major victory – the 2015 PGA Championship.

17. D – Matt Kuchar. At first, Kuchar only paid the caddie $5,000, but after receiving a tremendous amount of backlash, Kuchar paid him in full.

18. D – Rory McIlroy. McIlroy won the FedEx Cup in 2016 and then again in 2019. In 2016, he won the TOUR Championship in a playoff, while in 2019 it was by four strokes.

19. B – University of Texas. Spieth stayed local after going to high school in Dallas. He only played two years of golf collegiately before turning professional in 2012.

20. True. Thomas won the CIMB Classic in 2015 and 2016. This came before he won four times during the 2017 season, including the PGA Championship.

21. A – Alexander. Schauffele has won four times on the PGA Tour and was the 2017 Rookie of the Year.

22. False. Williams has caddied for Greg Norman, Raymond Floyd, Woods, Scott, Danielle Kang, and Jason Day, but never for Justin Rose.

23. C – California. Mickelson was born in San Diego and still lives in the area to this day. He attended college at Arizona State.

24. C – 5. Spieth won the Valspar, the Masters, the U.S. Open, the John Deere Classic, and the TOUR Championship in 2015.

25. B – Kevin Na. "I got done with the hole and I said (to my caddie), 'I think I made somewhere between a 10 and a 15,'" Na said afterwards. "But I think it's close to a 15." Nope, it was a 16.

26. B – Auburn. It's often there are a number of "War Eagle" chants tossed in Dufner's direction during some of his rounds.

27. D – Billy Horschel. It was quite the run for the Florida product. He finished second at the Deutsche Bank Championship and then won the BMW Championship and TOUR Championship in back-to-back weeks.

28. C – Dustin Johnson. The shot was so good that at the time, the Golf Channel's Brandel Chamblee called it his favorite shot in PGA Tour history.

29. A – Matthew Wolf. After starring at Oklahoma State, Wolf turned professional and made good use of his sponsors exemption by winning in his fourth career PGA Tour start.

30. True. Despite winning only one major (2016 U.S. Open), Johnson has played well in them. He finished second in the 2019 Masters and PGA Championship and then second at the 2011 British Open.

31. False. 2012 was one of McIlroy's best as a professional, as he claimed all of those titles. In addition, he helped Europe win the Ryder Cup.

32. False. Furyk won the 2010 FedEx Cup thanks to his one-stroke victory over Luke Donald at the TOUR Championship. Furyk entered the week No. 11 in the standings.

33. C – PGA Championship. Walker won the 2016 edition by one stroke over Jason Day.

34. False. Westwood actually went four straight years finishing third or better in at least one major. This was from 2008–11.

35. B –John Deere Classic. Spieth won the 2013 edition in a playoff over David Hearn and Zach Johnson. He won the event again in 2015.

36. C – 2014. Not only did McIlroy win the final two majors that year, he also won the WGC-Bridgestone Invitational sandwiched in the middle of them.

37. True. The left-hander has won the Masters in 2012 and 2014. Besides a second-place finish at the PGA Championship in 2010, the other three majors have not been kind to him.

38. A – Dustin Johnson. Johnson was the leading money winner that year and won twice, including the U.S. Open.

39. C – Oklahoma State. Fowler had an outstanding amateur career before he turned professional in 2009.

40. C – Winning FedEx Cup. Horschel won the 2014 FedEx Cup by winning the final two events of the series.

41. B – Kentucky. Despite growing up in the state of Kentucky, Thomas went to college at the University of Alabama. He now resides in Jupiter, Florida.

BLACK TEES

42. B – Waste Management Open. Koepka won the 2015 edition and then waited two more years for his next win, which came at the U.S. Open. While Koepka thrives at majors, his first tour win was not one.

43. B – Geoff Ogilvy. The Australian won the 2006 event and then won it again in 2009. The 2006 tournament was in California and the 2009 tournament was in Arizona.

44. True. Rahm won the Farmers Insurance Open in January of 2017 and then later that year won the Dubai Duty Free Irish Open.

45. D – 5. It is pretty remarkable that of Watson's 12 wins overall on the PGA Tour, five of them have come in playoffs. Overall, he is 5–1 in extra holes.

46. True. Despite being very successful on the PGA Tour, Oosthuizen's lone win came at the 2010 British Open. He has won nine times on the European Tour.

47. C – Keegan Bradley. Pat's brother and Keegan's father, Mark, is a PGA Professional in Wyoming.

48. A – Travelers Championship. It came in the final round where he went from being in 70th place at the start of the day, to finishing in a tie for fifth.

49. A – Luke Donald. Donald was the leading money winner that year where he won twice but did not capture a major.

50. B – Xander Schauffele. Schauffele won twice that year, including at the Greenbrier and then at the final event of the year—the TOUR Championship.

VI. TIGER WOODS

QUESTIONS

No single player in the history of the sport has meant as much as Tiger Woods. The television ratings prove it—when Woods is in the mix people tune in and when he isn't the vast majority of people don't.

When Woods was at his best in the 2000s, he simply dominated the sport. If he didn't win a tournament, it was a disappointment. And it wasn't like he would win by one or two strokes either, he blew the fields away.

Some courses even needed to become "Tiger proof," as the superstar had tremendous length where he would just overpower courses like no one else could and that gave him a tremendous advantage.

Of course, Woods has had his off-course issues, both health-related and personal, but the way he came back to not only win the TOUR Championship in 2018, but also the Masters in 2019 is something that could never be scripted. Those were two of the best moments in the history of the sport because of what Woods was able to overcome and how much fan support he had.

Simply put, there will never be a player that means more to the game than Woods.

"I'm aware if I'm playing at my best I'm tough to beat, and I enjoy that."

–Tiger Woods

"There's no sense in going to a tournament if you don't believe that you can win it. And that is the belief I have always had, and that is not going to change."

–Tiger Woods

Answers for this section are on pages 69–74.

RED TEES

1. What college did Tiger Woods attend?
   A. UCLA
   B. University of Arizona
   C. Stanford
   D. Texas

2. What is Tiger Woods's first name?
   A. Earl
   B. Eldrick
   C. Thomas
   D. Timothy

3. In 2009, after what holiday did Tiger Woods crash his car in front of his house and suffer minor face lacerations following reports of him having an affair?
   A. Fourth of July
   B. Labor Day
   C. Thanksgiving
   D. Christmas

4. What state did Tiger Woods grow up in?
   A. Florida
   B. Rhode Island
   C. California
   D. Texas

5. What body part has bothered Tiger Woods the most over his career?
A. Ankle
B. Back
C. Foot
D. Arm

6. What brand shirt does Tiger Woods always wear?
A. Nike
B. Callaway
C. Under Armour
D. Jordan

7. How many kids does Tiger Woods have?
A. 0
B. 1
C. 2
D. 3

8. What company has Tiger Woods not had an endorsement deal with?
A. McDonalds
B. American Express
C. Nike
D. Gatorade

9. True/False: Tiger Woods was honored by President Donald Trump in 2019 with the Presidential Medal of Freedom.

10. True/False: Tiger Woods once dated skier Lindsey Vonn.

WHITE TEES

11. Which tournament was Tiger Woods's first major?
A. Masters
B. British Open
C. PGA Championship
D. U.S. Open

12. Who was Tiger Woods's caddie in the late 90s before taking over on Jim Furyk's bag?
A. Steve Williams
B. Michael Greller
C. Mike Cowan
D. Jim Mackay

13. What year did Tiger Woods win the PGA Tour's Rookie of the Year?
A. 1989
B. 1996
C. 2000
D. 2002

14. Who did Tiger Woods beat to win the 2008 U.S. Open?
A. Rocco Mediate
B. Y.E. Yang
C. Bill Haas
D. Retief Goosen

15. What year did Tiger Woods win his first PGA Tour Player of the Year?
A. 1994
B. 1997
C. 1998
D. 2000

16. What is now known as the "Tiger Slam?"
   A. Holding all major titles at the same time although not in the same year
   B. Fist pump after making long putt
   C. Winning three out of four majors in same year
   D. Winning Masters and U.S. Open in back-to-back majors

17. True/False: Tiger Woods did not win a major in 2003 or 2004.

18. Who overtook Tiger Woods as world No. 1 in 2004?
   A. Rory McIlroy
   B. Vijay Singh
   C. Adam Scott
   D. David Duval

19. Which brand golf ball does Tiger Woods currently use?
   A. Nike
   B. Titleist
   C. TaylorMade
   D. Bridgestone

20. Which major did Tiger Woods win by 15 strokes in 2000?
   A. Masters
   B. U.S. Open
   C. British Open
   D. PGA Championship

21. Which tournament did Tiger Woods win in 2018, which was his first win since 2013?
   A. TOUR Championship
   B. BMW Classic
   C. Masters
   D. Wells Fargo

22. Of Tiger Woods's 15 majors, how many did he not have either a share of the lead or outright lead heading into final round?
A. 0
B. 1
C. 4
D. 5

23. How old was Tiger Woods when he played in his first Masters (1995)?
A. 18
B. 19
C. 21
D. 22

24. True/False: Tiger Woods has missed the cut in every major at least once.

25. True/False: Tiger Woods has played in at least one major every year since turning professional.

26. True/False: Tiger Woods has won every major by at least five strokes.

27. Tiger Woods holds the record for most lopsided victory in a match play event (2006). What was it?
A. 8&7
B. 9&8
C. 7&6
D. 6&5

28. Which one of Tiger Woods's swing coaches wrote a book on working with him?
A. Hank Haney
B. Sean Foley
C. Steve Williams
D. Chris Como

29. How are Tiger Woods and Notah Begay III so close?
A. Grew up on same street
B. Played college golf at Stanford together
C. Begay caddied for Woods early on in his career
D. Played tons of practice rounds early on in his career

30. True/False: Tiger Woods is into golf course design.

31. Who did Tiger Woods play in a match play event the day after Thanksgiving in 2018 streamed online?
A. Rory McIlroy
B. Phil Mickelson
C. Jordan Spieth
D. Ian Poulter

32. How many years did Tiger Woods play golf at Stanford?
A. 1
B. 2
C. 3
D. 4

33. What year did Tiger Woods become world No. 1 for the first time?
A. 1995
B. 1997
C. 1999
D. 2000

BLACK TEES

34. How old was Tiger Woods when he recorded his first hole in one?
A. 5
B. 8
C. 15
D. 20

35. True/False: Tiger Woods has never lost in a playoff.

36. When Tiger Woods made his remarkable chip-in for birdie on the sixteenth hole at the 2005 Masters, what was his status in the tournament at the time?
A. Tied for lead
B. Led by one
C. Down by one
D. Down by two

37. What year did Tiger Woods's dad pass away, a year in which he won six consecutive PGA Tour events?
A. 1998
B. 2000
C. 2006
D. 2008

38. Tiger Woods's current caddie Joe LaCava used to caddie for which pro?
A. Fred Couples
B. Tom Watson
C. Adam Scott
D. Paul Casey

39. How many playoffs has Tiger Woods been in during majors?
A. 0
B. 1
C. 3
D. 5

40. How many times has Tiger Woods won Player of the Year on the PGA Tour?
A. 5
B. 7
C. 8
D. 11

41. How many U.S. Amateurs did Tiger Woods win?
A. 0
B. 1
C. 3
D. 5

42. Who replaced Tiger Woods as the No. 1 golfer in 2010?
A. Rory McIlroy
B. Lee Westwood
C. Adam Scott
D. Ernie Els

43. Who was the runner-up in Tiger Woods's first major (1997 Masters)?
A. Ernie Els
B. David Duval
C. Tom Kite
D. Fred Couples

44. Why was Tiger Woods almost disqualified from the 2013 Masters?
   A. Used wrong ball by accident
   B. Took an illegal drop
   C. Played out of order
   D. Was late to tee time

45. What was Tiger Woods's record in the 2018 Ryder Cup?
   A. 2–2–0
   B. 3–0–1
   C. 2–2–0
   D. 0–4–0

46. True/False: Tiger Woods is an only child, but has two half-brothers and a half-sister.

47. True/False: Tiger Woods won the first tournament he played in following his father's death.

48. How many times has Tiger Woods won the Farmers Insurance Open?
   A. 2
   B. 4
   C. 5
   D. 7

49. True/False: Tiger Woods has never missed the cut at consecutive majors.

50. How many times has Tiger Woods won the Accenture Match Play Championship?
   A. 1
   B. 3
   C. 5
   D. 7

VI. TIGER WOODS

ANSWERS

RED TEES

1. C – Stanford. After being heavily recruited by all the college golf powerhouses, Woods enrolled at Stanford in the fall of 1994 and declared economics his major.

2. B – Eldrick. Woods's mother (Kultida) came up with Eldrick because it began with "E" (for Earl, his father) and ended with "K" (for Kultida).

3. C – Thanksgiving. Following the incident, Woods released a statement on his website where he took responsibility for what happened, calling it a "private matter" and crediting his wife, Elin Nordegren, for helping him from the car.

4. C – California. Woods was introduced to the sport before the age of two by his dad. Woods was able to beat his dad by age 11.

5. B – Back. Woods's back has bothered him significantly, and he's had multiple surgeries on it. He also was forced to withdraw from a few tournaments due to back pain.

6. A – Nike. Woods started his relationship with the company in 1996 and the company stuck by the golfer when other companies, such as

Gatorade and AT&T, dropped him when he was going through his personal issues off the course.

7. C – 2. Sam Alexis Woods was born in 2007 and then Charlie Axel Woods was born in 2009.

8. A – McDonalds.

9. True. Woods went to the White House to receive the award following winning the Masters.

10. True. The two were together for three years, but broke up in 2015.

WHITE TEES

11. A – Masters. Woods won the 1997 Masters by 12 strokes over Tom Kite. He shot 70–66–65–69 for a total score of 18-under par.

12. C – Mike Cowan. Cowan, better known as "Fluff," was Woods's caddie from 1996–99. He was on the bag for Woods's first major, which was their only major victory together.

13. B – 1996. Woods won twice that year—his first two career victories. He won October 6 at the Las Vegas Invitational and then October 20 at the Walt Disney World/Oldsmobile Classic.

14. A – Rocco Mediate. This may have been Woods's best major performance as he could barely walk at times and announced after the tournament he would need knee surgery. He birdied the 72nd hole to force a playoff and then beat Mediate the next day.

15. B – 1997. Woods won four tournaments that year and was the Tour's leading money winner.

16. A – Holding all major titles at the same time although not in the same year. This occurred when Woods won the 2000 U.S. Open, British Open, and PGA Championship and then won the 2001 Masters.

17. True. After winning the 2002 U.S. Open, Woods did not win another major until he won the 2005 Masters.

18. B – Vijay Singh. Singh took over as world No. 1 in September of 2004. It wasn't until the following March where Woods regained his No. 1 status.

19. D – Bridgestone. Woods used Nike for the majority of his career, but in December of 2016 he signed a multi-year deal with Bridgestone Golf.

20. B – U.S. Open. Woods simply blew away the field at Pebble Beach. He finished with a final score of 12-under and then there was a three-way tie for second place at plus-three.

21. A – TOUR Championship. While Justin Rose was the big winner that week by claiming the FedEx Cup, Woods won for the first time in over five years.

22. B – 1. Before the 2019 Masters, Woods had a share of the lead or was in the lead after 54 holes in all 14 of his major wins. He trailed three players by three strokes before coming back to win at Augusta in 2019.

23. B – 19. Woods finished in a tie for 41st and was the only amateur to make the cut.

24. True. In fact, Woods missed the cut in three of the four majors during 2015. His only missed cut at the Masters came in 1996, though.

25. False. Due to various injuries, Woods did not play in any majors during 2016 and 2017. This came following missing the cut in the last three majors of 2015.

26. True. Woods has won the Masters by twelve strokes, the U.S. Open by fifteen strokes, the British Open by eight strokes and the PGA Championship by five strokes.

27. B – 9&8. Woods crushed Stephen Ames in the event, which came after Ames talked a little bit of smack about Woods leading up to the match.

28. A – Hank Haney. Woods fired Haney in May of 2010 following a nearly six-year relationship. The book, *The Big Miss*, came out nearly two years later.

29. B – Played college golf at Stanford together. Begay was Woods's teammate at Stanford for one year before Begay turned professional in 1995.

30. True. In November 2006, Woods announced his intention to begin designing golf courses around the world. His first course was in Dubai.

31. B – Phil Mickelson. Mickelson beat Woods in 22 holes, finishing under the lights, to win the $9 million prize.

32. B – 2. Woods left college after his sophomore year and two golf seasons to turn professional.

33. B – 1997. Woods's first time as world No. 1 lasted for just a week. Woods overtook Greg Norman in June of 1997 and then Ernie Els took over for Woods a week later. Woods would reclaim it again later that summer.

BLACK TEES

34. B – 8. It was at the Heartwell Golf Course in Long Beach, California, but because Woods was so short, he didn't see it go in the hole.

35. False. Woods is 15–2 in playoffs with his losses coming to Billy Mayfair at the 1998 Nissan Open and Padraig Harrington at the 2006 Dunlop Phoenix.

36. B – Led by one. Woods's chip from well off the green went up the slope behind the hole and then slowly came back down towards it before hanging on the edge and, after a split second, dropping in.

37. C – 2006. Woods's father Earl was diagnosed with prostate cancer in 1998, but ultimately passed following suffering a heart attack at his home.

38. A – Fred Couples. LaCava and Couples actually won the 1992 Masters together.

39. C – 3. Woods defeated Bob May in the 2000 PGA Championship, Chris DiMarco in the 2005 Masters, and Rocco Mediate in the 2008 U.S. Open.

40. D – 11. Woods has won the PGA Tour Player of the Year in 1997, 1999, 2000, 2001, 2002, 2003, 2005, 2006, 2007, 2009, and 2013.

41. C – 3. Woods won the U.S. Amateur in three consecutive years (1994, 1995, and 1996).

42. B – Lee Westwood. After Woods was world No. 1 for a record 281 straight weeks, Westwood overtook him in October of 2010.

43. C – Tom Kite. Even more impressive for Woods in his 12-stroke rout was he was three strokes behind the leader following Round 1.

44. B – Took an illegal drop. Woods was assessed a two-stroke penalty for an illegal drop, which took place in the second round after hitting the ball in the water at the par-5 fifteenth hole. The infraction wasn't discovered until the following morning before the third round.

45. D – 0–4–0. Woods admitted afterwards he was mentally exhausted from the consecutive weeks he had played leading up to the event, which included him winning the TOUR Championship.

46. True. Woods has two half-brothers, Earl Jr. and Kevin, as well as a half-sister named Royce from his father's first marriage.

47. False. Woods missed the cut in the U.S. Open, but went on to win the British Open in his next major start.

48. D – 7. Woods has dominated the event held at Torrey Pines. He's won in 1999, 2003, 2005, 2006, 2007, 2008, and 2013.

49. False. Woods missed the cut in three of the four majors in 2015, but before then he did not miss consecutive cuts in majors.

50. B – 3. Woods captured this tournament in 2003, 2004, and 2008.

VII. MASTERS

QUESTIONS

There is no question the Masters is one of the biggest—if not the biggest—tournaments the players participate in each year. Even the average person who is not totally into golf will sit down and watch the back nine on Sunday.

It is unique compared to the other majors because it is hosted by the same course—Augusta National—each year, and yet it is a course every professional looks forward to playing every April. Scoring is fair, as there are quite a few holes where birdies can be had, but if players put themselves in bad spots they will certainly pay the price.

For some, especially in cold-weather states, the Masters is the official start of the golf season and really is a must-see event every single year.

"If there's a golf course in heaven, I hope it's like Augusta National. I just don't want an early tee time."

–Gary Player

"From the first time I drove up Magnolia Lane at age 19, I had a special feeling about Augusta. Even today, I get chills driving up Magnolia Lane."

–Jack Nicklaus

Answers for this section are on pages 85–90.

RED TEES

1. True/False: Augusta National is a public golf club.

2. The caddies at the tournament all wear the same color. What is it?
   A. Green
   B. Blue
   C. White
   D. Red

3. Who puts the famous green jacket on the winner of the Masters immediately following the tournament?
   A. Jack Nicklaus
   B. The previous champion
   C. Head of Augusta National
   D. PGA Tour commissioner

4. At the Masters in 2016, Jordan Spieth went into the back nine on Sunday with a five-stroke lead. What led to his collapse that ultimately lost him the tournament?
   A. Bogeyed five straight holes
   B. Hit two balls into the water on par-3 twelfth hole
   C. Hit two balls into water on par-5 fifteenth hole
   D. Lost his ball on the hole leading to triple bogey

5. What day is the finals of the Drive, Chip, & Putt event held at the Masters?
   A. Monday following the tournament
   B. Sunday preceding the tournament
   C. Wednesday of tournament week
   D. Tuesday of tournament week

6. True/False: No player has won the par-3 contest and the actual tournament in the same year.

7. True/False: Television coverage between ESPN and CBS shows every shot from the first tee shot to the last putt each day.

8. In 2019, how much was a domestic beer at the Masters?
   A. $4
   B. $6
   C. $8
   D. $12

9. How many par-5s are there at Augusta National?
   A. 2
   B. 3
   C. 4
   D. 5

10. True/False: There's a famous saying, "The Masters doesn't start until the back-nine on Sunday."

WHITE TEES

11. Who has won the most Masters tournaments with six?
   A. Arnold Palmer
   B. Tiger Woods
   C. Jack Nicklaus
   D. Gary Player

12. In 1935, Gene Sarazen make an albatross in the "shot heard 'round the world." Which hole was it on?
   A. Hole 2
   B. Hole 15
   C. Hole 13
   D. Hole 18

13. Who is the only player to complete the career Grand Slam at the Masters?
    A. Tiger Woods
    B. Gary Player
    C. Ben Hogan
    D. Gene Sarazen

14. Which player has won three or more Masters tournaments?
    A. Phil Mickelson
    B. Bubba Watson
    C. Tom Watson
    D. Ben Hogan

15. Tiger Woods and Jordan Spieth hold the record for the lowest score to win the tournament. What was it?
    A. 22-under
    B. 15-under
    C. 18-under
    D. 12-under

16. The low amateur gets an award at the end of the tournament. What is it called?
    A. Silver cup
    B. Green medal
    C. Bobby Jones medal
    D. Gold medal

17. True/False: Tiger Woods is the only player ever to win back-to-back Masters tournaments.

18. Which player has not won a Masters title?
    A. Angel Cabrera
    B. Fred Couples
    C. Danny Willett
    D. Louis Oosthuizen

19. Who was the first foreign-born player to win a Masters (in 1961)?
A. Gary Player
B. Roberto de Vicenzo
C. Angel Miguel
D. Seve Ballesteros

20. How many Masters did Arnold Palmer win?
A. 2
B. 4
C. 5
D. 6

21. Who was the first black player to compete in the Masters?
A. Tiger Woods
B. Lee Elder
C. Charlie Sifford
D. Ted Rhode

22. Who was the first Australian to win the Masters (in 2013)?
A. Greg Norman
B. Jason Day
C. Adam Scott
D. Marc Leishman

23. Who is the oldest Masters champion at age 46?
A. Ben Crenshaw
B. Tom Watson
C. Phil Mickelson
D. Jack Nicklaus

24. Who is the youngest player to win the Masters at age 21?
A. Jordan Spieth
B. Jack Nicklaus
C. Tiger Woods
D. Gary Player

25. Which golfer has blown the biggest 54-hole lead (six shots) and gone on to lose the Masters?
A. Fred Couples
B. Lee Westwood
C. Jordan Spieth
D. Greg Norman

26. What year was the first Masters held?
A. 1900
B. 1926
C. 1934
D. 1940

27. Which US president had a home at Augusta National?
A. Dwight D. Eisenhower
B. John F. Kennedy
C. Richard Nixon
D. Ronald Reagan

28. In the 2011 Masters, Rory McIlroy had a four-stroke lead heading into the final round, but he ultimately did not win the tournament. What did he shoot on Sunday?
A. 70
B. 74
C. 78
D. 80

29. Roughly how many players are in the Masters each year?
A. 90–100
B. 110–120
C. 125–130
D. 140–150

30. True/False: The winner of the Masters has always finished under par.

31. What was so unique about Nick Faldo's back-to-back Masters wins in 1989 and 1990?
    A. They were by five strokes or more
    B. Greg Norman was second in both
    C. Both came in playoffs
    D. He had three eagles in both final rounds

32. Who won their first major at the Masters in 2017 (playoff over Justin Rose)?
    A. Patrick Reed
    B. Sergio Garcia
    C. Danny Willett
    D. Rickie Fowler

33. Why was the Masters cancelled from 1943–45?
    A. Augusta National was being re-done
    B. World War II
    C. Concerns the course was too difficult
    D. The Masters has never been cancelled

34. True/False: Almost all playoffs at the Masters prior to 1976 were three aggregate holes.

35. Which network besides CBS and ESPN has provided Masters coverage over the years?
    A. FOX
    B. NBC
    C. ABC
    D. USA Network

BLACK TEES

36. What is not a name for a hole at Augusta National?
A. Magnolia
B. Cherry Blossom
C. Pink Dogwood
D. White Dogwood

37. Who won a sudden-death playoff with a bogey?
A. Adam Scott
B. Greg Norman
C. Patrick Reed
D. Mike Weir

38. Who was the first player to win the Masters in a sudden-death playoff?
A. Mike Weir
B. Greg Norman
C. Fuzzy Zoeller
D. Nick Faldo

39. Where is the sand in Augusta National's bunkers from?
A. Bermuda
B. North Carolina
C. Georgia
D. Florida

40. Who did Mike Weir beat in a playoff to win the 2003 Masters?
A. Tiger Woods
B. Len Mattiace
C. Retief Goosen
D. Jim Furyk

41. In 2009, which player recorded eleven birdies in the second round?
   A. Tiger Woods
   B. Phil Mickelson
   C. Adam Scott
   D. Anthony Kim

42. Which player has never won back-to-back Masters?
   A. Tiger Woods
   B. Nick Faldo
   C. Arnold Palmer
   D. Jack Nicklaus

43. Who won the first Masters playoff?
   A. Gene Sarazen
   B. Tom Watson
   C. Tom Kite
   D. Jack Nicklaus

44. How many Masters titles has Walter Hagen won?
   A. 0
   B. 1
   C. 2
   D. 3

45. True/False: Greg Norman has won two Masters titles.

46. How many Masters did Fred Couples play in before he missed his first cut (2019)?
   A. 20
   B. 23
   C. 27
   D. 33

47. Who made the longest putt in Masters history (100-plus feet)?
A. Nick Faldo
B. Rory McIlroy
C. Fred Couples
D. Gary Woodland

48. Who of the following was never the low amateur at the Masters?
A. Tiger Woods
B. Sergio Garcia
C. Jordan Spieth
D. Bryson DeChambeau

49. What is the best finish for an amateur at the Masters?
A. Win
B. Second place
C. Fifth place
D. 10th place

50. Who won the Masters in 2011?
A. Adam Scott
B. Bubba Watson
C. Phil Mickelson
D. Charl Schwartzel

VII. MASTERS

ANSWERS

RED TEES

1. False. Augusta National is one of the most exclusive clubs in the world and opened for play in 1932. It did not allow black players until 1990.

2. C – White. It's been a tradition for many years for the caddies to wear white jumpsuits. This isn't just for the Masters tournament, either.

3. B – The previous champion. Green jacket winners keep their jacket for the first year after their first victory then return it to the club to wear whenever they visit. This tradition began in the 1940s with Sam Snead.

4. B – Hit two balls into the water on the par-3 twelfth hole. Spieth made a quadruple bogey 7 on the hole, but rebounded with birdies on holes thirteen and fifteen. Ultimately, Danny Willett won by three strokes.

5. B – Sunday preceding the tournament. The Drive, Chip, & Putt is a joint initiative founded in 2013 by the Masters Tournament, United States Golf Association, and the PGA of America to grow the game with children.

6. True. The par-3 contest takes place the day before the tournament and typically is a family event with the players bringing their families onto the nine-hole, par-27 course on the Augusta National property.

7. False. Masters television coverage doesn't begin until the afternoon each day, although Masters.com provides extensive coverage of the tournament, including live streaming of certain groups and holes.

8. A – $4. Augusta National is known for its cheap concession prices. Sandwiches go for just $3.

9. C – 4. Holes two, eight, thirteen, and fifteen are all par-5s at Augusta National and more often than not are the difference come tournament week. Birdies can be had on all four holes.

10. True. Famous *Sports Illustrated* sports writer Dan Jenkins deserves credit for the saying.

WHITE TEES

11. C – Jack Nicklaus. Nicklaus won the Masters in 1963, 1965, 1966, 1972, 1975, and 1986. Tiger Woods has won the tournament five times, while Arnold Palmer has won it four times.

12. B – Hole 15. Sarazen holed a 4-wood from 235 yards out to record a very rare double eagle.

13. D – Gene Sarazen. Sarazen won the 1935 Masters to complete his career Grand Slam. It was his only Masters title.

14. A – Phil Mickelson. Mickelson has won the Masters three times: 2004, 2006, and 2010.

15. C – 18-under. Woods won the 1997 tournament with that score, while Spieth won the 2015 edition with it.

16. A – Silver Cup. In 1952, the Masters began presenting the low amateur with the award. The amateur must make the 36-hole cut to receive the award, though.

17. False. Jack Nicklaus won the Masters in 1965 and 1966, and Nick Faldo won it in 1989 and 1990.

18. D – Louis Oosthuizen. The South African has a decent track record, but has never won. His best finish was second in 2012.

19. A – Gary Player. The South African finished at 8-under par, which was one stroke ahead of Charles Coe and Arnold Palmer.

20. B – 4. Palmer won the Masters in 1958, 1960, 1962, and 1964.

21. B – Lee Elder. Elder played in the 1975 Masters, but missed the cut. He went on to win four times on the PGA Tour and another eight times on the Champions Tour.

22. C – Adam Scott. Greg Norman could have been the first Australian to win the event, but his best finish was second (three times).

23. D – Jack Nicklaus. When Nicklaus won his sixth and final Masters title in 1986, he was 46 years, 82 days old.

24. A – Jordan Spieth. When Spieth won in 2017 he was 21 years, 104 days old.

25. D – Greg Norman. Norman was dominating the 1996 event before he shot a final-round 76 and, by way of a 67, Nick Faldo came away with a five-stroke win at 12-under par.

26. C – 1934. Horton Smith won the first ever Masters with a 4-under final score, which gave him a two-stroke victory.

27. A – Dwight D. Eisenhower. There is even the famous Eisenhower tree on the seventeenth hole. The former US president didn't like the tree because it always got in the way of his left-to-right ball flight.

28. D – 80. It was not a good day at all for McIlroy, who actually finished the tournament in a tie for 15th place. Charl Schwartzel shot a final-round 66 to win by two strokes.

29. A – 90–100. It is one of the smaller fields, but this adds to its prestige.

30. False. Sam Snead won the 1954 edition, his third overall, with a score of plus-1.

31. C – Both came in playoffs. In 1989 he defeated Scott Koch and then the following year he defeated Raymond Floyd.

32. B – Sergio Garcia. This was Garcia's first major title, which came in his 74th attempt. He birdied the first playoff hole (18th) to come away with the win.

33. B – World War II. These are the only years since its inception the tournament has not been played.

34. False. Earlier playoffs at the Masters were contested over 18 holes on Monday. The first, in 1935, was actually 36 holes on Monday.

35. D – USA Network. The network began airing first and second-round coverage in 1982. It was the first ever cable coverage for one of the golf majors. ESPN took over in 2008.

BLACK TEES

36. B – Cherry Blossom. Each hole is named after a tree or shrub since the course was formerly a plant nursery.

37. D – Mike Weir. In 2003, Weir made a bogey five on the 18th, but it didn't matter because his opponent made a double-bogey six.

38. D – Fuzzy Zoeller. Zoeller won the 1979 event in a sudden-death playoff. Before 1976, the playoff format was 18 or 36 holes the following day.

39. B – North Carolina. The white sand primarily comes from the Spruce Pine mining area of the northwestern portion of the state, which is near the Blue Ridge mountains.

40. B – Len Mattiace. Both players finished the tournament at 7-under par, but Mattiace made a double-bogey on the first playoff hole.

41. D – Anthony Kim. Kim shot a 65, which was the low round of the day. The eleven birdies remains the record for birdies in a single round at the Masters.

42. C – Arnold Palmer. Although Palmer won the Masters four times, none of them came in back-to-back years.

43. A – Gene Sarazen. Sarazen beat Craig Wood in 1935, the only time in the event's history that the playoff was 36 holes.

44. A – 0. Although Hagen won 11 majors, he never won at Augusta National. His best finish was a tie for 11th in the 1936 event.

45. False. Norman has never won the Masters. He did finish second three times, though.

46. D – 33. Not only did Couples make the cut 33 straight times, he also finished in the top-10 eleven times.

47. A – Nick Faldo. The putt came on the second hole in the 1989 final round and was said to be over 100 feet.

48. C – Jordan Spieth. Woods was the low amateur in 1995, Garcia in 1999, and DeChambeau in 2016.

49. B – Second place. Three players have accomplished this—Frank Stranahan in 1947, Ken Venturi in 1956, and Charles Coe in 1961.

50. D – Charl Schwartzel. Schwartzel birdied the final four holes for a two-stroke victory over Adam Scott and Jason Day.

VIII. PGA CHAMPIONSHIP

QUESTIONS

The PGA Championship doesn't generate nearly as much buzz as the other three majors, but some good battles have still been had at the event over the years.

It isn't just PGA Tour professionals who get to play in the event. PGA Professionals from around the country can qualify, which truly makes it a tournament for all PGA Professionals.

The tournament usually has a wide range of scores depending on which course is played, but by in large good scores can be had and it is not typically a battle just to make par.

Of course, some of the game's best players have won PGA Championships, but there have also been quite a few surprise players as well.

"For me, the PGA definitely had a special place in my heart. For this to be my first one and have my dad here, and I know grandpa was watching at home. I was able to talk to him and that was pretty cool."

—Justin Thomas

"It's an amazing feeling, just the work that I've put into my game ever since I was a 12-year-old kid, to be able to stand in front of a crowd like this today and win a PGA Championship is pretty special."

–Jason Day

Answers for this section are on pages 103–108.

RED TEES

1. What is awarded to the winner of the tournament each year?
   A. Hogan trophy
   B. Walker cup
   C. Wanamaker trophy
   D. Palmer's prize

2. Which of the following months has the PGA championship never been played in?
   A. August
   B. May
   C. November
   D. March

3. True/False: A playoff in the PGA Championship is an 18-hole playoff the following day.

4. Which is not one of the possible qualifying criteria for the PGA Championship?
   A. 20 low scorers in the PGA Professional National Championship
   B. Winners of the last five Masters
   C. Winners of the last 10 U.S. Opens
   D. Low 15 scorers and ties from previous year's PGA Championship

5. Which of the following does not get a player into the PGA Championship?
   A. Every former winner of the PGA Championship
   B. Every former Masters champion
   C. Winners of the last three PLAYERS championships
   D. Low 15 scores (and ties) from the last PGA Championship

WHITE TEES

6. Who won the 2011 PGA Championship in a playoff?
   A. Tiger Woods
   B. Keegan Bradley
   C. Jason Day
   D. Jason Dufner

7. True/False: The PGA Championship has never had a winner finish the week over par.

8. Who has the record for the lowest 72-hole winning score at the PGA Championship?
   A. Tiger Woods
   B. Brooks Koepka
   C. Jason Day
   D. Jack Nickalus

9. Who is the oldest player to win the PGA Championship?
   A. Julius Boros
   B. Raymond Floyd
   C. Greg Norman
   D. Fred Couples

10. True/False: Pebble Beach has never hosted a PGA Championship.

11. True/False: The PGA Championship was once a match play tournament.

12. Who did Tiger Woods famously beat in a playoff at Valhalla during the 2000 PGA Championship?
    A. Bob May
    B. Steve Stricker
    C. Y.E. Yang
    D. Justin Leonard

13. Who is the youngest player to win the PGA Championship at 20 years old?
    A. Justin Thomas
    B. Jordan Spieth
    C. Tiger Woods
    D. Gene Sarazen

14. Which state has hosted the most PGA Championships?
    A. California
    B. Florida
    C. Ohio
    D. New York

15. What was so unique about John Daly's win in the 1991 PGA Championship?
    A. He was an alternate
    B. He used a golf cart
    C. It was completed on a Tuesday
    D. He won in an 18-hole playoff

16. Who won the 2009 PGA Championship, which was the first major Tiger Woods failed to win when leading after 54 holes?
A. Martin Kaymer
B. Y.E. Yang
C. Rich Beem
D. David Toms

17. Martin Kaymer won the 2010 PGA Championship, but which player led by three after three rounds before shooting an 81 on Sunday to not even finish in the top-10?
A. Nick Watney
B. Rory McIlroy
C. Jason Dufner
D. Camilo Villegas

18. Davis Love III's PGA Championship title is his only major. What year did it happen?
A. 1994
B. 1997
C. 2000
D. 2003

19. True/False: Jimmy Walker's PGA Championship win in 2016 was wire-to-wire.

20. The total field has a maximum of how many players?
A. 100
B. 125
C. 156
D. 206

21. How many strokes did Brooks Koepka lead by heading into the final round of the 2019 edition at Bethpage Black?
    A. 1
    B. 3
    C. 7
    D. He didn't have the lead

22. True/False: NBC once held the broadcast rights of the PGA Championship before CBS.

23. Who is the only player to win the PGA Championship in three different decades?
    A. Tiger Woods
    B. Jack Nicklaus
    C. Gary Player
    D. Gene Sarazen

24. True/False: The PGA Championship has been held at The Country Club in Brookline, Massachusetts, multiple times.

25. True/False: Jason Day became the first Australian to win the PGA Championship.

26. Which year did Sergio Garcia get national attention for his outgoing antics when he finished second to Tiger Woods at the PGA Championship?
    A. 1995
    B. 1999
    C. 2002
    D. 2004

27. Who was the runner-up for David Toms's PGA Championship in 2001?
    A. Tiger Woods
    B. Chad Campbell
    C. Phil Mickelson
    D. Sergio Garcia

28. True/False: Pinehurst has never hosted a PGA Championship.

29. In the 2010 PGA Championship, who did Martin Kaymer defeat in a playoff?
    A. Tiger Woods
    B. Jason Dufner
    C. Bubba Watson
    D. Jim Furyk

30. True/False: In the 1960s, there was never a repeat winner of the PGA Championship.

31. True/False: The PGA Championship has never been held in California.

32. When Tiger Woods defeated Bob May in three-hole aggregate playoff in 2000, how many birdies did he have in those holes?
    A. 0
    B. 1
    C. 2
    D. 3

33. True/False: There has never been "lift, clean, and place" (when players can pick their ball up in their own fairway and clean it before playing a shot, usually when courses are wet) at a PGA Championship.

34. Who of the following has never won a PGA Championship?
   A. Sergio Garcia
   B. David Toms
   C. Jimmy Walker
   D. Jeff Sluman

BLACK TEES

35. Which course has hosted the tournament the most times?
   A. Southern Hills Country Club
   B. Bethpage Black
   C. Winged Foot
   D. Pebble Beach

36. Jordan Spieth and Arnold Palmer are two players missing the PGA Championship for the career Grand Slam. Who is the third?
   A. Gary Player
   B. Tom Watson
   C. Greg Norman
   D. Sam Snead

37. Which player shot 76 in the final round and still won the 2004 PGA Championship?
   A. Phil Mickelson
   B. David Toms
   C. Rich Beem
   D. Vijay Singh

38. Which course hosted the 2001 and 2011 PGA Championship where David Toms and Keegan Bradley both won?
   A. Atlanta Athletic Club
   B. Whistling Straits
   C. Medinah CC
   D. Quail Hollow

39. Shaun Micheel won the 2003 PGA Championship. Which of the following players finished in the top five?

A. Phil Mickelson

B. Chad Campbell

C. Lee Westwood

D. Rich Beem

40. Who holds the record for largest margin of victory in the PGA Championship (eight strokes)?

A. Rory McIlroy

B. Tiger Woods

C. Vijay Singh

D. Nick Price

41. Who won the most PGA Championships when it was match play (five)?

A. Walter Hagen

B. Byron Nelson

C. Ben Hogan

D. Gene Sarazen

42. The lowest 18-hole score during the PGA Championship is a 63. Which of the following players have never recorded a 63 during the event?

A. Jason Dufner

B. Mark O'Meara

C. Brad Faxon

D. Rory McIlroy

43. Which player finished runner-up in the final year the PGA Championship when it was match play, but won the first year when it was stroke play?
A. Gary Player
B. Sam Snead
C. Dow Finsterwald
D. Doug Ford

44. Who has the most majors without winning a PGA Championship?
A. Tom Watson
B. Phil Mickelson
C. Jordan Spieth
D. Gary Player

45. Who was the first player to win consecutive PGA Championships?
A. Jim Barnes
B. Gene Sarazen
C. Tiger Woods
D. Tommy Armour

46. Who holds the PGA Championship record for greatest final-round comeback of seven strokes?
A. Arnold Palmer
B. Tom Watson
C. John Mahaffey
D. Raymond Floyd

47. Paul Azinger won the 1993 PGA Championship. Who did he defeat in a playoff?
A. Greg Norman
B. Tom Kite
C. Fred Couples
D. Tom Watson

48. True/False: None of Walter Hagen's five PGA Championship wins in match play needed extra holes.

49. In 2002, Tiger Woods birdied the final four holes of the tournament. What place did he come in?
A. First
B. Second
C. Third
D. Fifteenth

50. How many strokes did Jack Nicklaus win his fifth and final PGA Championship in 1980 by?
A. 1
B. 3
C. 5
D. 7

VIII. PGA CHAMPIONSHIP

ANSWERS

RED TEES

1. C – Wanamaker trophy. The trophy is 27 pounds and measures 28 inches high, 10.5 inches in diameter, and 27 inches from handle to handle, making it the largest trophy of the four majors.

2. C – March. No majors take place before the Masters in April. In the early days, the PGA Championship was a fall event and over the years has varied from May to December.

3. False. The PGA Championship uses a three-hole aggregate playoff system to determine the winner in the event of a tie.

4. C – Winners of the last 10 U.S. Opens. Winners of the last five U.S. Opens qualify, but not the last 10.

5. B – Every former Masters champion. All former Masters champions do not automatically get invites to the PGA Championship.

WHITE TEES

6. B – Keegan Bradley. Bradley defeated Dufner in the three-hole aggregate playoff with a one-under score. Dufner was even-par.

7. False. Four times the winner of the PGA Championship has finished with a score over par.

8. C – Jason Day. Day won the 2015 edition at Whistling Straits with a final score of 20-under par to beat Jordan Spieth by three strokes.

9. A – Julius Boros. Boros was 48 years, 142 days old when he won in 1968.

10. False. Pebble Beach hosted the 1977 edition when Lanny Watkins won in a playoff with a tournament score of six-under par.

11. True. The match play era lasted from 1916–1957.

12. A – Bob May. Woods and May finished the tournament at 18-under par and then Woods finished one-under in the three-hole playoff to beat May, who shot even-par.

13. D – Gene Sarazen. When Sarazen won the 1922 edition he was 20 years, 5 months, 22 days old.

14. D – New York. The state of New York has hosted thirteen PGA Championships, led by Oak Hill Country Club, which has hosted three.

15. A – He was an alternate. Daly got into the field at Crooked Stick as the ninth alternate and then won by three shots at 12-under par.

16. B – Y.E. Yang. Woods had an uncharacteristically bad Sunday when he shot 75 and Yang shot 70 to come away with a three-shot win. Woods led by two over Yang and Padraig Harrington going into the day.

17. A – Nick Watney. Watney had a three-stroke lead over Dustin Johnson and Rory McIlroy entering the day, but a crazy final round ended with Martin Kaymer defeating Bubba Watson in a playoff to win his first career major.

18. B – 1997. Love III shot a final round 66 for a five-stroke win over Justin Leonard at Winged Foot. Leonard had won the British Open just a month before.

19. True. Walker shot 65–66–68–67 to win by a single shot over Jason Day.

20. C – 156. The PGA Championship is the only all-professional major championship.

21. C – 7. Dustin Johnson closed the gap thanks to Koepka bogeying five of his last eight holes, but he was still able to come away with a two-stroke win.

22. False. ABC had the broadcast rights until 1991 before it moved to CBS.

23. B – Jack Nicklaus. Nicklaus won five PGA Championships – 1963, 1971, 1973, 1975, and 1980.

24. False. The PGA Championship has only been held in Massachusetts once and that was at Blue Hill Country Club.

25. False. The first Australian to win the PGA Championship was Jim Ferrier in 1947. He defeated Chick Harbert 2&1 in the final match.

26. B – 1999. He is most remembered for his shot in the final round when his ball was up against a tree trunk on the 16th hole. He swung with his eyes shut and hit a low curving fade that ran up onto the green. Garcia sprinted up the fairway and jumped high enough to see the result over a hill.

27. C – Mickelson. Toms finished the tournament at 15-under, one stroke ahead of Mickelson. Toms had a two-shot lead heading into the day and was never really challenged by anyone but Mickelson.

28. False. The 1936 edition was played at Pinehurst No. 2. It was won by Denny Shute and he also won the following year.

29. C – Bubba Watson. In a back-and-forth three-hole aggregate playoff, Kaymer won by a stroke. Watson's bogey on the last was the difference.

30. True. 1960–1969 saw 10 different winners, including Gary Player and Jack Nicklaus.

31. False. The event has been held in California four times with a fifth coming in 2020.

32. B – 1. Woods birdied the first aggregate hole, the sixteenth, where he walked the ball into the cup and pointed for one of his most famous celebrations on the course.

33. False. Most recently, when Jimmy Walker won in 2016 at Baltusrol there was "lift, clean, and place" for the final round.

34. A – Sergio Garcia. Garcia has only won a major once, and that was the 2017 Masters. He's been the runner-up at the PGA Championship twice—1999 and 2008.

BLACK TEES

35. A – Southern Hills Country Club. Designed by Perry Maxwell, this course has hosted the PGA Championship four times—1970, 1982, 1993, and 2007.

36. B – Tom Watson. Watson has won eight majors, but never the PGA Championship. His best finish is a tie for second in 1978.

37. D – Vijay Singh. The 76 was the highest ever final round score by a PGA champion. Scoring conditions were very tough, as all the leaders shot in the 70s.

38. A – Atlanta Athletic Club. In 2001, Toms beat Phil Mickelson by one stroke and then in 2011, Bradley beat Jason Dufner by one in a three-hole aggregate playoff.

39. B – Chad Campbell. There really wasn't much star-power in the top-five at this tournament. Campbell finished second, Tim Clark third, and Alex Čejka fourth.

40. A – Rory McIlroy. McIlroy blew away the field at Kiawah Island. Unknown David Lynn finished in second.

41. A – Walter Hagen. Hagen won in 1921 and then won four straight from 1924–1927.

42. D – Rory McIlroy. In all, 17 players have shot 63s during the PGA Championship.

43. C – Dow Finsterwald. Finsterwald lost 2&1 to Lionel Herbert in 1957 and then won by two strokes the following year with Billy Casper coming in second place.

44. A – Tom Watson. Watson has won eight majors, but doesn't have a PGA Championship to his name, which is preventing him from the career Grand Slam. His best finish was a tie for second in 1978.

45. A – Jim Barnes. Barnes won the first two PGA Championships, which were held in 1916 and 1919. The event wasn't held in 1917 and 1918 because of World War I.

46. C – John Mahaffey. Tom Watson shot a 73 to give up a five-shot lead he had going into the final round. Mahaffey beat Watson and Jerry Pate in a playoff.

47. A – Greg Norman. Azinger birdied four of the last seven holes to get into the playoff and then won on the second hole. Norman three-putted from 20 feet to bogey, while Azinger two-putted for par.

48. True. Hagen dominated, winning the tournament five times in the 1920s, but none of them went extra holes. He was the runner-up in 1923 and that went 38 holes.

49. B – Second. Rich Beem won the tournament by a stroke over Woods, although he bogeyed 18 knowing that would still win the tournament.

50. D – 7. Nicklaus was the only player to finish under par in the event. He finished at 6-under, while Andy Bean was the runner-up at plus-1.

IX. U.S. OPEN

QUESTIONS

Any player who wins the U.S. Open certainly deserves it, as it typically is the hardest major. Par is a good score as the courses are set up to really challenge the players in all facets. Typically, the event is played at long courses, not to mention narrow fairways and very, very thick rough.

There have even been some years where the USGA, who is in charge of the event, gets criticized by fans and players for making the course too hard.

Also, unlike the PGA Championship, the event isn't just for PGA Tour professionals, as this one is more for amateurs. There are sectional qualifiers all over the country, so it really is a case where anyone in America has the chance to qualify.

This tournament has seen some of the greatest moments in the sport's history and really is one of a kind.

"A difficult golf course eliminates a lot of players. The U.S. Open flag eliminates a lot of players. Some players just weren't meant to win the U.S. Open. Quite often, a lot of them know it."
–Jack Nicklaus

"The U.S. Open has never been exciting to watch. It has always been a sad tournament. There is no excitement, no enjoyment. It is all defensive golf, from the first tee to the last putt."
–Seve Ballesteros

Answers for this section are on pages 121–126.

RED TEES

1. True/False: The U.S. Open playoff format is 18 holes on Monday.

2. Which network took over TV coverage of the U.S. Open in 2015?
   A. CBS
   B. ESPN
   C. FOX
   D. Golf Channel

3. What is the U.S. Open trophy called?
   A. The U.S. Open trophy
   B. The Palmer trophy
   C. The American Champion trophy
   D. The Sarazen cup

4. The 2004 U.S. Open at Shinnecock Hills was criticized for the course set-up. Why?
   A. Course length
   B. Rough was too long
   C. Greens were too firm and couldn't hold shots
   D. Fairways were too narrow

5. Which of the following does not qualify a player for the U.S. Open?
   A. Top 10 finishers and ties from the previous U.S. Open
   B. Winner and runner-up from previous year's U.S. Amateur
   C. Winner and runner-up from previous five Masters and PGA Championships
   D. Winner of the previous U.S. Senior Open

WHITE TEES

6. Which of the following courses has hosted the U.S. Open?
   A. Beverly Golf & Tennis
   B. The Country Club
   C. Trump National
   D. TPC Sawgrass

7. True/False: The winning score of the U.S. Open has never been over par in back-to-back years.

8. How many U.S. Opens has Hale Irvin won?
   A. 0
   B. 1
   C. 3
   D. 5

9. Who is the oldest player to win the U.S. Open (45 years old)?
   A. Craig Stadler
   B. Hale Irwin
   C. Raymond Floyd
   D. Tom Watson

10. There are two players to shoot 63 in the final round of the U.S. Open. One of them is Johnny Miller. Who is the other?
    A. Adam Scott
    B. Justin Thomas
    C. Tommy Fleetwood
    D. Tiger Woods

11. True/False: There has never been a U.S. Open winner who hasn't shot at least one round in the 60s.

12. There are four players who have the most U.S. Open titles (four). Who is not one of them?
A. Ben Hogan
B. Willie Anderson
C. Bobby Jones
D. Hale Irwin

13. Which of the following players has not won the U.S. Open multiple times?
A. Andy North
B. Ernie Els
C. Lee Janzen
D. Phil Mickelson

14. Where was the first U.S. Open held?
A. Newport Country Club
B. Bethpage Black
C. Pebble Beach
D. Shinnecock Hills

15. Dustin Johnson won the 2016 U.S. Open, but what happened in the final round that was the story of the tournament afterwards?
A. Rory McIlroy shot 62
B. Johnson was assessed a one-stroke penalty for making his ball move as he addressed it on fifth green
C. Johnson lost his ball on eighteen, but still was able to win
D. Tiger Woods shot 65

16. At Chambers Bay in 2015, Jordan Spieth won by one stroke, but it was an unlikely result. Why?

    A. Dustin Johnson three-putted from 12 feet when he needed to two-putt for 18-hole playoff

    B. Spieth holed out from eighteenth fairway for eagle

    C. Johnson needed to take an unplayable after his tee shot on eighteen and made bogey

    D. Louis Oosthuizen shot 79 in the final round after leading by five

17. True/False: Angel Cabrera's win at the 2007 U.S. Open was the first by a South American.

18. True/False: From 2010–14, four out of the five U.S. Open winners were European.

19. True/False: Ben Hogan's four U.S. Open titles came in a six-year span.

20. Who is the only player to have a combined score under par in any of the three U.S. Opens won by Tiger Woods?

    A. Ernie Els

    B. Rocco Mediate

    C. Matt Kuchar

    D. Lee Westwood

21. Who had the lowest world ranking of any U.S. Open champion?

    A. Michael Campbell

    B. Angel Cabrera

    C. Steve Jones

    D. Lucas Glover

22. Before Brooks Koepka, who was the last player to win back-to-back U.S. Opens?
A. Tiger Woods
B. Curtis Strange
C. Hale Irvin
D. Ben Hogan

23. True/False: An amateur has never won the U.S. Open.

24. True/False: The 2015 U.S. Open at Chambers Bay had holes one and eighteen switch back-and-forth between par-4s and par-5s.

25. The 2003 U.S. Open was held at Olympia Fields. What state is that in?
A. New York
B. Pennsylvania
C. Illinois
D. California

26. True/False: Pebble Beach has hosted the most U.S. Opens with nine.

27. Who won the U.S. Open in 1990 after receiving a special exemption?
A. Hale Irwin
B. Johnny Miller
C. Davis Love III
D. Lee Trevino

28. Who is the youngest U.S. Open winner (age 19)?
A. Jordan Spieth
B. John McDermott
C. Tommy Bolt
D. Bobby Jones

29. True/False: The state of Maryland has never hosted the U.S. Open.

30. Who has played in the most consecutive U.S. Opens (44)?
A. Sam Snead
B. Arnold Palmer
C. Jack Nicklaus
D. Bobby Jones

31. True/False: ABC has aired the U.S. Open at some point over the years.

32. True/False: The U.S. Open has not been played every year since 1900.

BLACK TEES

33. Who is the youngest player to make the cut at the U.S. Open (since World War II, 17 years old)?
A. Tiger Woods
B. Jordan Spieth
C. Beau Hossler
D. Rory McIlroy

34. What is the record for most strokes under par at any point during the U.S. Open?
A. 10-under par
B. 13-under par
C. 15-under-par
D. 17-under par

35. Who is the only player to win the U.S. Open in three straight years?
A. Bobby Jones
B. Walter Hagen
C. Willie Anderson
D. Jack Nicklaus

36. Who was in the final group of the U.S. Open for three straight years, but never won?
A. Lee Westwood
B. Tom Lehman
C. Jim Furyk
D. Greg Norman

37. Who has lost the U.S. Open in a playoff three times?
A. Arnold Palmer
B. Jack Nicklaus
C. Phil Mickelson
D. Sam Snead

38. In the second round of the 1989 U.S. Open at Oak Hill Country Club, how many hole-in-ones were recorded on the par-3 sixth hole?
A. 2
B. 3
C. 4
D. 6

39. Martin Kaymer won the 2014 U.S. Open at Pinehurst No. 2 by how many strokes?
A. In a playoff
B. 1
C. 4
D. 8

40. In the 1966 U.S. Open, Billy Casper erased a seven-stroke deficit on the final nine holes and then beat Arnold Palmer in an 18-hole playoff at which course?
A. Pinehurst No. 2
B. The Olympic Club
C. Pebble Beach
D. The Country Club

41. How many strokes did Payne Stewart win the 1999 U.S. Open by?
A. 1
B. 3
C. 5
D. 6

42. Three players finished three strokes behind Lucas Glover at the 2009 U.S. Open. Who was one of the three?
A. Matt Kuchar
B. Jim Furyk
C. Mike Weir
D. Ricky Barnes

43. Who has been the runner-up at the U.S. Open the most times?
A. Greg Norman
B. Arnold Palmer
C. Phil Mickelson
D. Lee Westwood

44. In the 2005 U.S. Open at Pinehurst No. 2, Retief Goosen, Jason Gore, and Olin Browne were the top three players after 54 holes. What did they all have in common on Sunday?
A. They all shot in the 60s, but lost
B. They all failed to break 80
C. They all hit approach shots to eighteen in water
D. They all missed their tee times due to traffic

45. Who is the last U.S. Open winner to not break par in any round?

A. Michael Campbell

B. Corey Pavin

C. Lee Janzen

D. Geoff Ogilvy

46. Only one player has ever won the U.S. Open twice at the same course. Who is it?

A. Tiger Woods

B. Curtis Strange

C. Jack Nicklaus

D. Davis Love III

47. Who was the first player in U.S. Open history to shoot all four rounds in the 60s?

A. Jack Nicklaus

B. Ben Hogan

C. Lee Trevino

D. Arnold Palmer

48. Which of the following courses has hosted at least four U.S. Opens?

A. Myopia Hunt Club

B. Bethpage Black

C. Trump National

D. Whistling Straits

49. Who holds the record for most consecutive top-25 finishes in the U.S. Open (19)?

A. Tiger Woods

B. Walter Hagen

C. Jack Nicklaus

D. Ben Hogan

50. Retief Goosen defeated Mark Brooks in 2001 to win the U.S. Open in a playoff. How did it get there?

A. Brooks eagled eighteen on Sunday

B. Goosen three-putted for bogey on eighteen on Sunday

C. Brooks shot 65 to tie Goosen on Sunday

D. Goosen chipped in on eighteen on Sunday

IX. U.S. OPEN

ANSWERS

RED TEES

1. False. The playoff format was 18 holes on Monday until a 2018 change, which now has it as a two-hole aggregate playoff.

2. C – FOX. The 2019 edition featured a total of 38 hours of coverage in the United States, with 20 hours being on Thursday and Friday, and 18 hours being on Saturday and Sunday. Before 2015, NBC and ESPN had the rights.

3. A – The U.S. Open trophy. It does not have a real name and is a silver trophy that has two handles on the sides of a silver jug on top of a silver base.

4. C – Greens were too firm and couldn't hold shots. At one point, officials watered the par-3 seventh green during play to try and make it more fair for players to hold shots on the green.

5. C – Winner and runner-up from previous five Masters and PGA Championships. While the winners from the last five Masters and PGA Championships get into the U.S. Open, the runners-up do not.

WHITE TEES

6. B – The Country Club. This famous course in Brookline, Massachusetts, has hosted the tournament three times—1913, 1963, and 1988.

7. False. The winning score has been over par a number of times, including most recently in 2012 and 2013.

8. C – 3. Irvin won the U.S. Open in 1974, 1979, and 1990. These three wins are his only majors.

9. B – Hale Irwin. When Irwin won in 1990 he was 45 years and 15 days old.

10. C – Tommy Fleetwood. Fleetwood shot 63 in 2018 at Shinnecock, but it wasn't enough to win. He finished one shot behind Brooks Koepka, who shot two-under in the final round.

11. False. This has happened a number of times, including Geoff Ogilvy in 2005 when he shot 71–70–72–72 to win at Winged Foot.

12. D – Hale Irwin. Irwin only won the tournament three times.

13. D – Phil Mickelson. The lefty hasn't won the U.S. Open at all, which is keeping him from the career Grand Slam. He has finished second six times, though.

14. A – Newport Country Club. This club hosted the first U.S. Open in 1895 and was won by Horace Rawlins.

15. B – Johnson was assessed a one-stroke penalty for making his ball move as he addressed it on fifth green. It didn't really matter much, as Johnson still won the tournament by three strokes.

16. A – Dustin Johnson three-putted from 12 feet when he needed to two-putt for 18-hole playoff. Spieth was ready for a playoff, but Johnson's issue on the eighteenth green gave him his second career major.

17. True. Cabrera's win at Oakmont was the first U.S. Open won by a South American or Argentine.

18. True. Graeme McDowell, Rory McIlroy, Webb Simpson, Justin Rose, and Martin Kaymer were the winners during those years with Simpson being the only player not from Europe.

19. True. Hogan's wins came from 1948–1953.

20. B – Rocco Mediate. Mediate finished at one-under par. In Woods's other two wins, the runner-up was even par.

21. C – Steve Jones. Jones was ranked No. 99 when he won in 1996.

22. B – Curtis Strange. Strange won the event in 1988 and 1989.

23. False. The U.S. Open has been won by an amateur a few times— Johnny Goodman (1933), Bobby Jones (1926), and Jerome Travers (1915).

24. True. The first hole was a par-4 and the eighteenth a par-5 for three of the four rounds. Friday was the only day the first hole was a par-5 and eighteen a par-4.

25. C – Illinois. Jim Furyk was the winner, as he finished at 8-under par—three strokes ahead of Stephen Leaney.

26. False. Oakmont Country Club has hosted the most U.S. Opens with nine. Pebble Beach has hosted the event six times.

27. A – Hale Irwin. Irwin needed a special exception from the USGA as he hadn't won on the PGA Tour in over five years and was eleven years removed from his last U.S. Open victory in 1979.

28. B – John McDermott. In 1911, McDermott was 19 years, 9 months, and 14 days old when he won the event.

29. False. The state of Maryland has hosted the U.S. Open five times—three times at Congressional Country Club, once at Baltimore Country Club, and once at Columbia Country Club.

30. C – Jack Nicklaus. From 1957–2000, Nicklaus played in 44 straight U.S. Opens and won four of them.

31. True. ABC had the rights to the tournament from 1966–1994.

32. True. The event was cancelled in 1917 and 1918 due to World War I and again from 1942–1945 due to World War II.

BLACK TEES

33. C – Beau Hossler. Hossler made the cut at age 17 in 2012. He actually had a share of the lead briefly, but ended up by finishing tied for 29th.

34. D – 17-under par. McIlroy was 17-under during the final round of the 2011 edition. His winning score was 16-under—an eight-stroke win.

35. C – Willie Anderson. Anderson won the tournament in 1903, 1904, and 1905.

36. B – Tom Lehman. Lehman was the 54-hole leader of the U.S. Open from 1995–1997, but failed to win each time.

37. A – Arnold Palmer. Palmer lost in playoffs in 1962, 1963, and 1966. He did win the event in 1960.

38. C – 4. Doug Weaver, Mark Wiebe, Jerry Pate, and Nick Price all recorded holes-in-one within a two-hour span.

39. D – 8. Kaymer blew the field away finishing with a final score of 9-under par. Rickie Fowler and Eric Compton finished in second place at 1-under par.

40. B – The Olympic Club. There were only fifteen sub-par rounds posted and four belonged to Billy Casper.

41. A – 1. Stewart won by one stroke over Phil Mickelson and it came a year after he lost a four-stroke lead after 54 holes in the 1998 U.S. Open.

42. D – Ricky Barnes. In addition to Barnes, David Duval and Phil Mickelson also finished three strokes behind Glover.

43. C – Phil Mickelson. Mickelson has finished second in the U.S. Open six times—1999, 2002, 2004, 2006, 2009, 2013.

44. B – They all failed to break 80. Goosen, who had a three-shot lead going into the day, shot 81 and finished tied for 11th. Gore shot 84 and finished in a tie for 49th. Browne shot 80 and finished tied for 23rd.

45. D – Geoff Ogilvy. Ogilvy came away with the win in a wild final round. Runners-up Colin Montgomerie, Jim Furyk, and Phil Mickelson all failed to par the 18th hole and finished one stroke behind.

46. C – Jack Nicklaus. Nicklaus won the 1967 edition at Baltusrol as well as the 1980 edition.

47. C – Lee Trevino. Trevino shot rounds of 69–68–69–69 to finish at 5-under par, four strokes better than Jack Nicklaus.

48. A – Myopia Hunt Club. It was a popular course in the early days, hosting the 1898, 1901, 1905, and 1908 editions.

49. B – Walter Hagen. Hagen finished in the top 25 from 1913–16 and then 1919–33 (there were no championships 1917–18).

50. B – Goosen three-putted for bogey on eighteen on Sunday. In the playoff, Goosen shot even-par, while Brooks came in at plus-2.

X. BRITISH OPEN

QUESTIONS

The fourth and final major may be the most unique. It is played primarily in England and Scotland, which have courses that are much different than those in the United States. These courses are much more open and do not have much water but have a ton of deep bunkers. The weather also plays much more of a factor.

Usually, there's wind and some rain, which impacts scores a great deal. On the flip side, if there is no wind or rain, the courses are pretty gettable and good scores can be had.

This tournament has been won by some of the best players in the world, but also has had some surprising champions. Players must adapt to the links style, and that is why there are a variety of winners.

Typically, the better ball-strikers are the ones who do the best in this tournament, as well as players who can shape their ball with wind being a factor. There is also a ton of history at almost all of the venues.

Getting up early in the United States to watch this tournament live is usually rewarded with some terrific storylines, as well as very competitive golf.

> *"It may be years before I fully appreciate it, but I am inclined to believe that winning The Open at the Home of Golf is the ultimate achievement in the sport."*
>
> –Tiger Woods

"If you're going to be a player people will remember, you have to win the Open at St. Andrews."

–Jack Nicklaus

Answers for this section are on pages 137–141.

RED TEES

1. What did the winner of the first British Open receive?
   A. Championship belt
   B. Claret jug
   C. Red jacket
   D. Crown

2. True/False: The British Open rotates between three courses: St. Andrews, Carnoustie, and Royal Troon.

3. Which British Open course is the oldest course in the world?
   A. Royal Portrush
   B. St. Andrews
   C. Turnberry
   D. Royal Liverpool

4. What are British Open courses most known for?
   A. Fast greens
   B. Lots of water
   C. Pot bunkers
   D. Tree-lined fairways

5. True/False: No amateurs are allowed to compete.

6. True/False: Typically, every round begins on the first tee, not split between the first and tenth.

7. Who is under authority of the British Open?
   A. USGA
   B. European Tour
   C. R&A
   D. PGA Tour

WHITE TEES

8. Where did Tiger Woods win his first British Open?
   A. St. Andrews
   B. Royal St. George's
   C. Royal Liverpool
   D. Carnoustie

9. Which player won the British Open in his first start at a major championship?
   A. Tiger Woods
   B. Jordan Spieth
   C. Ben Curtis
   D. Greg Norman

10. True/False: Tom Morris Sr. holds the greatest victory margin of thirteen.

11. The 2002 British Open was decided by a four-man playoff. Who won?
   A. Steve Elkington
   B. Ernie Els
   C. Payne Stewart
   D. John Daly

12. What was Ben Curtis's world ranking when he won the British Open in 2003?
A. 150
B. 250
C. 300
D. 396

13. True/False: John Daly won the 1995 British Open in a playoff.

14. The famous "Road Hole" is at which British Open course?
A. St. Andrews
B. Royal Troon
C. Royal Birkdale
D. Carnoustie

15. In 1999, Jean van de Velde stepped to the par-four eighteenth with a three-shot lead in the final round. What score did he post on that eighteenth hole?
A. 8
B. 3
C. 10
D. 7

16. True/False: The British Open has only been played outside England and Scotland twice.

17. Who has the most second-place finishes with seven?
A. Jack Nicklaus
B. Lee Westwood
C. Justin Rose
D. Arnold Palmer

18. True/False: The winner gets a five-year membership to the PGA and European Tours.

19. Who was the first American to win the event?
A. Arnold Palmer
B. Sam Snead
C. Bobby Jones
D. Jock Hutchison

20. When Todd Hamilton beat Ernie Els in a playoff in 2004, he saved par from 40 yards away by getting up and down with what club?
A. Putter
B. Driver
C. 4 iron
D. Hybrid

21. True/False: Scotland has hosted the tournament more than any other country.

22. How many British Opens has Tom Watson won?
A. 2
B. 3
C. 4
D. 5

23. True/False: The winner of the British Open started getting paid in American dollars beginning in 2017.

24. True/False: Tiger Woods has never finished in second place at the British Open.

25. Why was the 1988 third round cancelled?
A. Rain flooded the course
B. Too windy
C. Volunteers went on strike
D. Hurricane was making landfall just south of the course

26. How many strokes did Louis Oosthuizen win the 2010 British Open by?
A. 1
B. 2
C. 5
D. 7

27. Which player shot 63 in the final round to win the 2016 British Open?
A. Henrik Stenson
B. Justin Rose
C. Jordan Spieth
D. Zach Johnson

28. True/False: Nick Faldo won back-to-back British Opens in the late 1980s.

29. In 2009, Tom Watson led the British Open through 71 holes and had a chance to become oldest champion at 59 years old. What happened?
A. He made par and won
B. He made double bogey to lose
C. He made bogey and lost in a playoff
D. He made birdie and still lost

30. True/False: The British Open has been held every year since 1900.

31. True/False: Nick Faldo has more British Opens than Rory McIlroy.

32. Who was the first South African to win the British Open?
A. Ernie Els
B. Louis Oosthuizen
C. Bobby Locke
D. No one ever has

BLACK TEES

33. What was so unusual about Nick Faldo's final round when he won at Muirfield in 1987?
   A. He eagled the final hole to win
   B. He made three straight bogeys to close out round
   C. He had a hole in one
   D. He made 18 pars

34. Who is the only player to win the British Open at five different courses?
   A. Tiger Woods
   B. Old Tom Morris
   C. Tom Watson
   D. Harry Vardon

35. Who has the most wins of all-time with six?
   A. Tiger Woods
   B. Jack Nicklaus
   C. Harry Vardon
   D. Old Tom Morris

36. In 1983, which player famously missed a three-inch putt and eventually finished one stroke behind winner Tom Watson?
   A. John Daly
   B. Seve Ballesteros
   C. Tom Kite
   D. Hale Irwin

37. Which golfer won three straight British Opens in the 1950s?
   A. Peter Thomson
   B. Gary Player
   C. Ben Hogan
   D. Arnold Palmer

38. Who was the first player to win the British Open while ranked No. 1 in the world?
A. Nick Faldo
B. Tiger Woods
C. Rory McIlroy
D. Tom Watson

39. Which American golfer once called St. Andrews "the worst piece of mess" he'd ever seen?
A. Scott Hoch
B. Tom Lehman
C. Dustin Johnson
D. Justin Thomas

40. Since 1938, what was the highest score in relation to par to win the British Open?
A. Plus-4
B. Plus-8
C. Plus-12
D. Plus-21

41. The British Open had its first four-hole aggregate playoff in 1989. It was eventual champion Mark Calcavecchia, Greg Norman, and which other golfer?
A. Wayne Grady
B. Colin Montgomerie
C. Tom Lehman
D. Mark O'Meara

42. In 1980, the British Open did what for the first time?
A. Let American players into the field
B. Finished on a Sunday
C. Played 36 holes Saturday and Sunday
D. Allowed caddies

43. The first British Open champion from overseas came from which country?
A. Australia
B. United States
C. France
D. Canada

44. Who has appeared in the most British Opens (46 times)?
A. Jack Nicklaus
B. Gary Player
C. Tom Watson
D. Mark O'Meara

45. True/False: Justin Leonard's only major was the 1997 British Open.

46. How many British Opens did Seve Ballesteros win?
A. 2
B. 3
C. 4
D. 6

47. Who did Tom Watson go back-and-forth with to win the 1977 British Open?
A. Gary Player
B. Henry Cotton
C. Jack Nicklaus
D. Roger Maltbie

48. When John Daly won the 1995 British Open, what was his position heading into the final round?
A. Tied for lead
B. Ahead by one
C. Trailing by one
D. Trailing by four

49. Why was Prestwick Golf Club banned from hosting the British Open?
A. Couldn't handle number of spectators
B. Too easy of course
C. Conditions were poor
D. Flooding ruined course and was never repaired

50. Who holds the record for lowest score after 54 holes in British Open history (197)?
A. Tiger Woods
B. Henrik Stenson
C. Shane Lowry
D. Tom Watson

X. BRITISH OPEN

ANSWERS

RED TEES

1. B – Claret jug. The current claret jug was first awarded to Walter Hagen for winning the 1928 edition. The winner must return the trophy before the next year's tournament and receives a replica to keep permanently.

2. False. A total of fourteen courses have hosted the British Open and right now there are ten courses in the rotation.

3. B – St. Andrews. The course was originally built in 1552 and is known as "the home of golf."

4. C – Pot bunkers. British Open courses typically have hundreds of bunkers, which give players plenty of trouble. There are even times where players have to chip out of them sideways because they are so deep.

5. False. Amateurs are allowed to compete and there is a similar qualifying structure to the U.S. Open with local qualifying followed by a final qualifier.

6. True. Since there is more daylight in England and Scotland, split tees do not need to be used.

7. C – R&A. The R&A is the ruling authority of golf around the world, except in North America.

WHITE TEES

8. A – St. Andrews. Woods won the 2000 British Open by eight strokes with a final score of 19-under par.

9. C – Ben Curtis. Curtis won the 2003 edition at Royal St. George's by one stroke over Vijay Singh and Thomas Bjorn.

10. True. Morris Sr. won by thirteen strokes in 1862, the third edition of the tournament.

11. B – Ernie Els. Els and Thomas Levet needed sudden-death following the four-hole aggregate and Els made par, while Levet made bogey.

12. D – 396. Following the win, Curtis jumped from 396 to 35th. Going into the tournament, he had 300–1 odds to win.

13. True. Daly defeated Costantino Rocca in the aggregate playoff (1-under to 3-over) to win his first and only British Open.

14. A. St. Andrews. The seventeenth hole is one of the most famous holes at all of the British Open courses and players from the back tees cannot see where their tee shots land.

15. D – 7. Van de Velde made a triple-bogey and then played the four-hole aggregate playoff in plus-3 to lose to Paul Lawrie, who shot even-par.

16. True. Royal Portrush in Northern Ireland has hosted the event twice, but other than that it's been played exclusively in England and Scotland.

17. A – Jack Nicklaus. While Nicklaus has the most runner-up finishes, he's also won the event three times.

18. True. Other benefits include guaranteed entry to all future British Opens until the age of 60.

19. D – Jock Hutchison. Although he was born in Scotland, the 1921 winner was an American citizen when he won.

20. D – Hybrid. These clubs were just becoming popular around this time and received a ton of publicity following Hamilton's win.

21. True. It has hosted the event almost double the number of times as England.

22. D – 5. Watson has claimed victory in 1975, 1977, 1980, 1982, and 1983. In addition, he led the event after 54 holes in 2009.

23. True. Prior to 2017, the winner was paid in pounds.

24. True. While Woods has won the event three times, he has never been the runner-up.

25. A – Rain flooded the course. This was the first time in 27 years a full round was cancelled at the British Open. The tournament finished on Monday for the first time ever.

26. D – 7. Oosthuizen blew the final away, finishing with a score of 16-under par.

27. A – Henrik Stenson. With his final-round 63, Stenson won by three strokes over Phil Mickelson, who shot a final-round 65.

28. False. While Faldo has three Open Championships, none of them came in back-to-back years.

29. C – He made bogey and lost in a playoff. Stewart Cink beat Watson in the four-hole aggregate playoff, as he shot 2-under to Watson's 4-over.

30. False. The tournament was cancelled from 1915–19 due to World War I and then from 1940–45 due to World War II.

31. True. Faldo has won the event three times, while McIlroy has only won it once.

32. C – Bobby Locke. The South African won the event four times, including in back-to-back years (1949–50).

BLACK TEES

33. D – He made 18 pars. Faldo's even-par round was able to give him a one-stroke win.

34. C – Tom Watson. Watson's five wins came between 1975–83.

35. C – Harry Vardon. Vardon's wins came in 1896, 1898, 1899, 1903, 1911, and 1914.

36. D – Hale Irwin. Irwin essentially whiffed on a putt in the third round on the fourteenth hole, which ultimately cost him a chance at a playoff with Watson.

37. A – Peter Thomson. Thomson won the tournament five times, including all three years from 1954–56.

38. B – Tiger Woods. This occurred at the 2000 edition, which allowed Woods to earn the career Grand Slam.

39. A – Scott Hoch. Because of the comment, Hoch has been called an "ugly American" by Europeans.

40. D – Plus-21. In 1947, Fred Daly was the winner when he finished at plus-21, one stroke ahead of two golfers.

41. A – Wayne Grady. Grady led by one stroke entering the day, but then shot plus-1 in the playoff to fall to Calcavecchia.

42. B – Finished on a Sunday. Before 1980, the tournament started on a Wednesday and ended on a Saturday.

43. C – France. In 1907, Arnaud Massy won the tournament. Prior to that, the winners were exclusively from England or Scotland.

44. B – Gary Player. Despite playing in the event 46 times, Player has only won it twice.

45. True. Leonard shot 65 in the final round, which gave him a three-stroke victory.

46. B – 3. Ballesteros won the tournament in 1979, 1984, and 1988.

47. C – Jack Nicklaus. The two were paired together for the final two rounds and ran away from the field. Watson finished at 12-under, while Nicklaus was at 11-under. The third-place finisher was at 1-under.

48. D – Trailing by four. Daly shot a final round 71 to sneak into a playoff and defeat Costantino Rocca.

49. A – Couldn't handle number of spectators. The last time it hosted the event was 1925.

50. C – Shane Lowry. Lowry shot a final-round 72 to finish at 15-under par and win the tournament by six strokes.

XI. RYDER CUP/ PRESIDENTS CUP

QUESTIONS

These team events are some of the most entertaining in all of golf. When playing for their countries, players play with much more emotion and the match play formats add into it. The atmospheres are also some of the best in the sport with the fans feeding off the players' emotions. This even leads to the crowd taunting players from the visiting country.

When players discuss these events, the majority of them say it is the most nervous they have ever been on a golf course since they are not only representing their team, but also their country. There are also a massive number of people around the first tee to kick off each match adding to the pressure.

Some players are able to feed off the pressure and play some of their best golf, while others cannot handle it and play some of their worst golf.

Overall, the Europeans have dominated the United States in the Ryder Cup, while the United States has dominated the world in the Presidents Cup.

"Ryder Cup, Presidents Cup, whatever it may be, is maybe the most fun couple weeks we have a year, but I love being able to control my own destiny. The work that I am able to put in ahead of time was either going to come out and I was going to be

successful with it, or I was going to try and fail and learn how to succeed the next time."

–Jordan Spieth

"Any time I can get in front of the crowd, and especially the Americans, and have the red, white, and blue on, it just fuels me."

–Patrick Reed

Answers for this section are on pages 153–156.

RED TEES

1. True/False: The Ryder Cup is a tournament held every four years between teams from the United States and Europe.

2. True/False: The Ryder Cup does not have a stroke play portion.

3. What will the 1999 Ryder Cup at The Country Club in Brookline, Massachusetts, most be remembered for?
   A. Colin Montgomerie's last Ryder Cup
   B. Justin Leonard's 45-foot birdie putt on the 17th that won the United States the cup
   C. Tiger Woods's Ryder Cup debut
   D. The sportsmanship showed by both teams

4. At the 2017 Presidents Cup, Phil Mickelson took a selfie that went viral. Who was in it?
   A. The United States team and their wives
   B. Tiger Woods chugging beer
   C. President Bill Clinton, President George W. Bush, President Barack Obama
   D. Paulina Gretzky

5. Which country has produced the most players on the International team?

A. Australia

B. Japan

C. South Africa

D. Fiji

WHITE TEES

6. Which year did the Presidents Cup begin?

A. 1975

B. 1980

C. 1990

D. 1994

7. True/False: European players can compete in the Presidents Cup.

8. What year was the Ryder Cup founded?

A. 1960

B. 1975

C. 1890

D. 1927

9. Who is the youngest player ever to play in a Ryder Cup?

A. Rory McIlroy

B. Tiger Woods

C. Sergio Garcia

D. Jordan Spieth

10. The 1969 Ryder Cup came down to the final match and final hole with Tony Jacklin facing Jack Nicklaus. It ended up being a halved match and tied overall, which meant the United States retained the cup. Nicklaus received some criticism for how it ended. Why?
A. He bogeyed the par-5
B. He conceded a short birdie putt to halve the hole/match
C. He didn't shake Jacklin's hand afterwards
D. He stepped in Jacklin's line on purpose

11. Which American did Seve Ballesteros have issues with in the 1989 Ryder Cup where rules officials were called in multiple times in their Sunday singles match?
A. Paul Azinger
B. Hale Irvin
C. Davis Love III
D. Lee Trevino

12. One of the greatest comebacks in Ryder Cup history was in 1999 at The Country Club in Brookline, Massachusetts, when the United States won 14½–13½. What were they trailing going into Sunday?
A. 9–7
B. 10–6
C. 11–5
D. 12–4

13. Which side won the "Miracle at Medinah" in 2012?
A. United States
B. Europe
C. It was halved
D. There was never a "Miracle at Medinah"

14. True/False: Tiger Woods's Ryder Cup record is below .500.

15. Who has been the United States Ryder Cup captain the most times?
A. Paul Azinger
B. Ben Hogan
C. Walter Hagen
D. Davis Love III

16. Who has been the European Ryder Cup captain the most times?
A. Tony Jacklin
B. Darren Clarke
C. Dai Rees
D. John Jacobs

17. Which United States pairing was very successful in 2016, but did not get paired again in 2018, creating a lot of controversy among the media?
A. Tiger Woods and Dustin Johnson
B. Rickie Fowler and Justin Thomas
C. Jordan Spieth and Patrick Reed
D. Justin Thomas and Dustin Johnson

18. True/False: There is no prize money awarded at the Presidents Cup.

19. Who has recorded the most points in Presidents Cup history?
A. Tiger Woods
B. Greg Norman
C. Phil Mickelson
D. Adam Scott

20. The Presidents Cup was held at the same course for four of the first six events. Which course was it?
A. Royal Melbourne
B. Robert Trent Jones Golf Club
C. Bethpage Black
D. Medinah Country Club

21. True/False: The first Ryder Cup was held in Massachusetts.

22. Who has never been a U.S. Ryder Cup captain?
A. Corey Pavin
B. Tom Lehman
C. Hal Sutton
D. Tiger Woods

23. True/False: The Ryder Cup has never been held on the West Coast of the United States.

24. True/False: Tiger Woods has never halved a Ryder Cup match.

25. True/False: There's yet to be a hole-in-one during a Presidents Cup match.

BLACK TEES

26. The Ryder Cup is named after English businessman Samuel Ryder who made most of his money selling what?
A. Garden seeds
B. Gold
C. Wheat
D. Beer

27. Who has served as the U.S. captain in the Presidents Cup four times?
A. Hale Irvin
B. Jack Nicklaus
C. Jim Furyk
D. Fred Couples

28. Which player has the most Ryder Cup appearances of all-time?
A. Hale Irvin
B. Davis Love III
C. Phil Mickelson
D. Bernhard Langer

29. Who is the oldest player to compete in the Ryder Cup?
A. Raymond Floyd
B. Colin Montgomerie
C. Jack Nicklaus
D. Curtis Strange

30. From 2002–18, how many Ryder Cups did the United States win (out of 9)?
A. 0
B. 2
C. 4
D. 8

31. In 2015, the United States won the Presidents Cup 15 ½–14 ½. Which American clinched the cup on the final hole of the final match?
A. Bill Haas
B. Jordan Spieth
C. Patrick Reed
D. Phil Mickelson

32. True/False: In the Presidents Cup, Jack Nicklaus has been the United States captain four times and Gary Player was the International captain all four times.

33. The event was created and organized by what organization?
A. PGA Tour
B. European Tour
C. USGA
D. R&A

34. Why did many national media members leave on the eve of the last day of the 1996 Presidents Cup?
A. The United States had already won
B. They went on strike against the PGA Tour
C. They were kicked out by the players
D. Tiger Woods was leading the Quad City Classic

35. Which player became known as "Aquaman" for falling face first into a water hazard after hitting a shot?
A. Woody Austin
B. Bill Haas
C. Frank Nobilo
D. Steve Elkington

36. Who is the oldest European to play in a Ryder Cup?
A. Dai Rees
B. Colin Montgomerie
C. George Duncan
D. Ted Ray

37. Which United States Ryder Cup player has won the most overall matches?
A. Arnold Palmer
B. Phil Mickelson
C. Tiger Woods
D. Billy Casper

38. In the 2006 Ryder Cup, there were two hole-in-ones, one by Paul Casey and the other by which American?
A. Tiger Woods
B. Phil Mickelson
C. Scott Verplank
D. Davis Love III

39. Which United States pairing has been the most successful in a single Ryder Cup?
A. Jim Furyk and Tiger Woods
B. Larry Nelson and Lanny Watkins
C. Fred Couples and Davis Love III
D. Steve Stricker and Tiger Woods

40. Who is the oldest International player to play in a Presidents Cup (49 years old)?
A. Nick Price
B. Vijay Singh
C. Greg Norman
D. Masashi Ozaki

XI. RYDER CUP/ PRESIDENTS CUP

ANSWERS

RED TEES

1. False. The Ryder Cup is held every two years, not every four years.

2. True. Friday and Saturday feature fourballs and foursomes and Sunday has single matches. Everything is match play.

3. B – Justin Leonard's 45-foot birdie putt on the seventeenth that won the United States the cup. This may be one of the most iconic moments in Ryder Cup history. Players and wives ran onto the green to celebrate even though Europe had a putt to keep that match alive.

4. C – President Bill Clinton, President George W. Bush, President Barack Obama. This occurred on the first tee before Mickelson teed off.

5. A – Australia. Australia leads the way by having almost nearly double the number of players than South Africa has had.

WHITE TEES

6. D – 1994. It was held at the Robert Trent Jones Golf Club and the United States came away with a 20–12 win.

7. False. The Presidents Cup features the United States against the rest of the world, minus Europe.

8. D – 1927. The first edition of the event was held in Worcester, Massachusetts, and Europe dominated, coming away with a 9.5–2.5 win.

9. C – Sergio Garcia. Garcia represented Europe in 1999 when he was just 19 years, 8 months, and 15 days old.

10. B – He conceded a short birdie putt to halve the hole/match. "I don't think you would have missed it, but I wasn't going to give you the chance, either," Nicklaus told Jacklin.

11. A – Paul Azinger. Early in the match Azinger didn't like Ballesteros wanting to take a scuffed ball out of play and then on the 18th hole, Ballesteros thought Azinger illegally dropped a ball. Azinger won the match, but Europe won the cup.

12. B – 10–6. The United States won the first six matches of the day to help them pull off the stunning upset.

13. B – Europe. It trailed 10–6, but staged a huge comeback, which included winning the first five singles matches.

14. True. Going into the 2020 Ryder Cup, Woods has a career record of 13–17–3.

15. C – Walter Hagen. Hagen was the United States captain for the first six editions of the event.

16. C – Dai Rees. Rees captained the European team five times— 1955, 1957, 1959, 1961, and 1967.

17. C – Jordan Spieth and Patrick Reed. Instead, Spieth was with Justin Thomas and Reed was with Tiger Woods.

18. True. The net proceeds are distributed to charities nominated by the players and captains.

19. C – Phil Mickelson. Mickelson has totaled 32.5 points, which includes a 26–16–13 record.

20. B – Robert Trent Jones Golf Club. It was held there in 1994, 1996, 2000, and 2005, but has not been held there since.

21. True. In 1928, it was hosted by Worcester Country Club.

22. D – Tiger Woods. One day that will likely change, but as of now Woods has never been a Ryder Cup Captain.

23. False. In the 1950s, it was held at Eldorado Golf Club and Thunderbird Country Club in California.

24. False. Woods has halved three matches. His record is 13–21–3.

25. True. While Jordan Spieth famously made a hole-in-one during a practice round in 2013, there has yet to be one in a live round.

BLACK TEES

26. A – Garden seeds. Ryder came up with the idea of Britain taking on the United States in a golf match and that is how the event was formed.

27. B – Jack Nicklaus. Nicklaus's record as captain was 2–1–1.

28. C – Phil Mickelson. The lefty has appeared in the Ryder Cup eleven times.

29. A – Raymond Floyd. In 1993, Floyd was 51 years and 20 days old.

30. B – 2. During this time, the United States won in 2008 and 2016.

31. A – Bill Haas. It was fitting because Bill's dad Jay was team captain.

32. False. When Nicklaus was captain for the first time in 1998, Peter Thomson was the International captain.

33. A – PGA Tour. Each event also has an honorary captain and it is typically a president or prime minister.

34. D – Tiger Woods was leading the Quad City Classic. This was a very competitive event with the United States leading by a point heading into the final day and held on for a one-point victory.

35. A – Woody Austin. This occurred at the 2007 Presidents Cup.

36. D – Ted Ray. In 1927, Ray was 50 years and 67 days old.

37. A – Arnold Palmer. Palmer has won six singles matches, nine foursomes, and seven fourballs to total 22 matches won overall.

38. C – Scott Verplank. Verplank's came in Sunday singles, while Casey's came in foursomes.

39. B – Larry Nelson and Lanny Watkins. This pairing won four points out of four in the 1979 event. It is the only pairing ever to do this for the United States.

40. D – Masashi Ozaki. In 1996, Ozaki was 49 years and 233 days old when he competed.

XII. AMATEUR TOURNAMENTS

QUESTIONS

While it doesn't generate much attention or buzz, all of the top golfers go through the amateur ranks before they reach the PGA Tour.

The U.S. Amateur is the biggest event, but even that doesn't get a lot of attention. In the last several years, college golf has become more popular with the NCAA Championships getting televised, but it isn't even close to what regular Tour events get.

Despite people not acknowledging it much, amateur events are still vital to the growth of the game and its winners have gone on to be the biggest names in the sport.

"Winning three Amateurs in a row is just something else. I just can't tell you what a weird feeling it is. I don't know what the significance is of this yet. I didn't know what the significance of winning two in a row was. It's going to take me awhile, that's for sure."

–Tiger Woods

"Having my name etched on this trophy with the great Bob Jones as well as Jack Nicklaus, Tiger Woods, Phil Mickelson, all those

guys, it's incredible. I can't even imagine what I just did. It won't sink in, I'm sure, for the next couple days. But I'm honored."

— Bryson DeChambeau

Answers for this section are on pages 163–165.

RED TEES

1. True/False: Amateurs are not allowed to claim prize money.

2. True/False: The U.S. Amateur combines both stroke and match play.

3. True/False: Jordan Spieth won two NCAA individual titles.

WHITE TEES

4. True/False: Bobby Jones won more U.S. Amateurs than Tiger Woods.

5. Which famous amateur golf trophy was named in honor of the grandfather of a former United States president?
   A. Walker Cup
   B. Johnson trophy
   C. Kennedy Cup
   D. Nixon trophy

6. The winner of the U.S. Amateur gets what of the following?
   A. Membership on the PGA Tour for the next season
   B. An invite to the Masters in the following year
   C. An invite to the PLAYERS Championship in the following year
   D. A lifetime invitation to the U.S. Amateur

7. The Walker Cup is an event between which countries?
A. United States and Australia
B. United States, United Kingdom, and Ireland
C. Great Britain and Ireland
D. United States and Great Britain

8. Which of the following players never won a U.S. Women's Amateur?
A. Lydia Ko
B. Danielle Kang
C. Morgan Pressel
D. Lexi Thompson

9. What college has the most NCAA golf team titles but hasn't won since the 1980s?
A. Yale
B. Houston
C. Wake Forest
D. UCLA

10. Which of the following players has won more than two NCAA individual titles?
A. Tiger Woods
B. Bryson DeChambeau
C. Phil Mickelson
D. Matt Kuchar

11. Which month is the U.S. Amateur typically played?
A. April
B. June
C. August
D. November

12. How many holes is the final match in the U.S. Amateur?
A. 9
B. 18
C. 27
D. 36

BLACK TEES

13. What year was the first U.S. Amateur contested?
A. 1895
B. 1925
C. 1945
D. 1950

14. Two players have won the U.S. Amateur and the U.S. Public Links in the same year. Of the following players, who is one of them?
A. Tiger Woods
B. Matt Kuchar
C. Ryan Moore
D. Jerry Pate

15. Who has the most Walker Cup appearances for the United States with nine?
A. Jordan Spieth
B. Francis Ouimet
C. Bobby Jones
D. Jay Sigal

16. What trophy does the winner of the U.S. Women's Amateur receive?
A. Gold ball trophy
B. Robert Cox cup
C. Ben Hogan trophy
D. Sam Snead cup

17. How old is the youngest winner of the U.S. Women's Amateur (Kimberly Kim)?
  A. 14
  B. 16
  C. 18
  D. 20

18. Which of the following players has never won an NCAA individual title?
  A. Luke Donald
  B. Ryan Moore
  C. Justin Thomas
  D. Aaron Wise

19. True/False: TPC Sawgrass has never hosted a U.S. Amateur.

20. Who has the most U.S. Amateur titles out of the following players?
  A. Tiger Woods
  B. Jerome Travers
  C. Jack Nicklaus
  D. Walter Travis

XII. AMATEUR TOURNAMENTS

ANSWERS

RED TEES

1. True. The rule states, "an amateur golfer may not accept a symbolic prize of any value."

2. True. The tournament consists of two days of stroke play, then the top 64 players advance to match play.

3. False. Spieth never won an NCAA individual title.

WHITE TEES

4. True. Jones won the tournament five times, while Woods won it three times.

5. A – Walker Cup. The trophy is competed for in odd-numbered years by amateur golfers in two teams.

6. B – An invite to the Masters in the following year. The winner and runner-up get invitations to the Masters for the following year.

7. B – United States, Great Britain, and Ireland. The Walker Cup was founded in 1922 and began with the U.S. taking on Great Britain, but has expanded since.

8. D – Lexi Thompson. Ko won it in 2012, Kang in 2010 and 2011, and Pressel in 2005.

9. B – Houston. It has been NCAA champions 16 times, but its last title came in 1985.

10. C – Phil Mickelson. The lefty was the NCAA individual champion in 1989, 1990, and 1992 while playing for Arizona State.

11. C – August. The event is hosted by various prestigious courses around the country.

12. D – 36. After stroke play, match play matches are 18 holes until the final match, which is 36 holes played on the same day.

BLACK TEES

13. A – 1895. It was held at the Newport Country Club where Charles B. Macdonald became the first champion. He won 12&11 over Charles Sands.

14. C – Ryan Moore. Moore won the U.S. Public Links in 2002 and 2004 and the U.S. Amateur in 2004.

15. D – Jay Sigal. Sigal competed in the event every year it was held from 1977–93.

16. B – Robert Cox cup. This has been awarded to the winner since 1896 and was donated by Robert Cox, a famous golf designer from Scotland.

17. A – 14. In 2006, Kim won the event when she was 14. She was also the runner-up at the 2006 and 2009 U.S. Women's Amateur Public Links.

18. C – Justin Thomas. Donald was champion in 1999, Moore in 2004, and Wise in 2016.

19. False. The course hosted the event in 1994 when Tiger Woods won for the first time.

20. B – Jerome Travers. Travers has won the event four times. Woods and Travis have won it three times.

XIII. PGA TOUR

QUESTIONS

The PGA Tour is the highest level of golf in the United States, and arguably the world since many players come over from the European Tour to play in a handful of events.

The Tour holds tournaments not only across the United States, but has expanded to around the world, most recently in Asia. Some of the tournaments have been around for dozens of years, while others have just begun.

With the exception of November and December, there is an event almost every week. Obviously some events are bigger than others, but the Tour has grown exponentially over the years. Some stops have even turned into must-see tournaments no matter who is competing in them.

The popularity of the Tour has also grown over the years for a number of reasons, including players being active on social media, more ways to watch (streaming, live television, etc.), and also more stars in the game making each tournament extremely competitive.

"(Hole 16) going to be pretty wild. It seems like every year it gets crazier and crazier. But it's so hard to control your adrenaline, you have so many juices pumping and your kind of like hands are tingling and it's a little shaky. It's just, it's a great atmosphere, it's a great hole. The fans are unbelievable; they are what makes this event what it is."

—Justin Thomas on Waste Management Open

"The playoffs are the biggest, besides the majors, are the four biggest events we have on the PGA Tour and that's when the light shines the brightest, and I was able to rise to the occasion and get the job done. And it just gives me so much confidence, so much thrill to accomplish something like this, especially with the guys I was going up against."

–Billy Horschel

Answers for this section are on pages 177–181.

RED TEES

1. What tournament is considered the "fifth major?"
   A. The PLAYERS Championship
   B. Arnold Palmer Invitational
   C. The Memorial
   D. AT&T Pebble Beach Pro/Am

2. True/False: The PGA Tour has an annual match play tournament.

3. From 2007–2018, the FedEx Cup consisted of four tournaments. How many are there now?
   A. Three
   B. Two
   C. Five
   D. Six

4. Which tournament is known for having the rowdiest fans on Tour?
   A. The PLAYERS
   B. Waste Management Open
   C. Arnold Palmer Invitational
   D. The Memorial

WHITE TEES

5. In what state is the Arnold Palmer Invitational held?
   A. Ohio
   B. Georgia
   C. North Carolina
   D. Florida

6. Which tournament typically follows the Masters?
   A. Wells Fargo
   B. RBC Heritage
   C. Valero Texas Open
   D. RBC Canadian Open

7. What is the name of the tournament that has been held in Hartford, Connecticut, for many years?
   A. Northern Trust
   B. Travelers Championship
   C. Dell Technologies Championship
   D. Wells Fargo

8. Which tournament annually comes before the British Open?
   A. John Deere Classic
   B. Wyndham Championship
   C. RBC Canadian Open
   D. Travelers Championship

9. Which month does Hawaii typically host two tournaments?
   A. December
   B. January
   C. May
   D. November

10. Which of the following players has won the FedEx Cup?
    A. Bill Haas
    B. Jon Rahm
    C. Sergio Garcia
    D. Adam Scott

11. What tournament does Jack Nicklaus and his family host on an annual basis?
    A. PLAYERS Championship
    B. Valspar Championship
    C. Memorial Tournament
    D. Northern Trust

12. What state does the Farmers Insurance Open typically take place in?
    A. California
    B. Kentucky
    C. Texas
    D. Ohio

13. Who won back-to-back money titles in 2017 and 2018?
    A. Brooks Koepka
    B. Justin Thomas
    C. Rory McIlroy
    D. Dustin Johnson

14. True/False: David Duval never won a PGA Tour money title.

15. True/False: The "West Coast Swing" typically takes place early in the season.

16. What makes the Sentry Tournament of Champions in Hawaii so special?
    A. Only major winners get invites
    B. Only PGA Tour tournament winners from the previous year get invites
    C. Winner gets invite to all four majors that year
    D. Only top 50 players in world get invites

17. True/False: An event is considered official after 54 holes.

18. What state is the PGA Tour headquarters in?
    A. California
    B. New York
    C. Oregon
    D. Florida

19. Which tournament at PGA National has the finishing holes that are known as "The Bear Trap?"
    A. The Honda Classic
    B. Arnold Palmer Invitational
    C. Valspar Championship
    D. Genesis Open

20. Which PGA Tour tournament during the summer features teams of two?
    A. Wells Fargo Championship
    B. Zurich Classic of New Orleans
    C. Rocket Mortgage Classic
    D. Barracuda Championship

21. The WGC match play event was held in Arizona for six years before going to Harding Park in California for a year in 2015. What state has the event been held in ever since?
    A. Arizona
    B. Texas
    C. Florida
    D. Oregon

22. True/False: The PGA Tour hosts official tournaments in Europe.

23. True/False: There are multiple PGA Tour events in Canada during the course of the year.

24. Winning any PGA Tour event gets you what?
    A. Lifetime membership on the tour
    B. A tour card for at least two years
    C. An invitation to the Masters for the following year
    D. An invitation to the PGA Championship for the following year

25. True/False: The PLAYERS Championship has had an identical point allocation as all four majors since the FedEx Cup began in 2007.

26. What state is the AT&T Byron Nelson tournament held?
    A. Florida
    B. Texas
    C. California
    D. Illinois

27. True/False: The PGA Tour has an official tournament in Japan.

28. What makes the World Golf Championships so special?
   A. They are match play events
   B. They offer comparable prize money to majors
   C. They have more players than typical PGA Tour events
   D. They are winners-only events

29. Who has won the most World Golf Championships?
   A. Tiger Woods
   B. Phil Mickelson
   C. Dustin Johnson
   D. Darren Clarke

BLACK TEES

30. Which year did the FedEx Cup start?
   A. 2000
   B. 2005
   C. 2007
   D. 2012

31. Who was the PGA Tour commissioner before Jay Monahan?
   A. Tim Finchem
   B. Joseph Dey
   C. Deane Beman
   D. Jimmy Walker

32. What PGA Tour season was the last to be conducted entirely within a calendar year?
   A. 2010
   B. 2013
   C. 2015
   D. 2018

33. Who was the first PGA Tour commissioner?
A. Joe Dey
B. Tim Finchem
C. Arnold Palmer
D. Jack Nickalus

34. How many money titles did Vijay Singh win?
A. 0
B. 1
C. 2
D. 3

35. Which course hosts the Genesis Open, formerly the Northern Trust Open, in January?
A. Pebble Beach
B. Riviera Golf Club
C. TPC Scottsdale
D. Torrey Pines

36. True/False: Mark O'Meara has the same number of AT&T Pebble Beach Pro-Am wins as Phil Mickelson (5).

37. How many tours does the PGA Tour operate?
A. 1
B. 2
C. 4
D. 6

38. Which of the following PGA tournaments is not considered an invitational-based tournament and does not follow the normal PGA Tour exemption categories?
A. RBC Heritage
B. Charles Schwab Challenge
C. Travelers Championship
D. Memorial Tournament

39. What year was the AT&T Byron Nelson established?
- A. 1944
- B. 1985
- C. 1990
- D. 2005

40. What year did the 3M Open originate?
- A. 2004
- B. 2010
- C. 2014
- D. 2019

XIII. PGA TOUR

ANSWERS

RED TEES

1. A – The PLAYERS Championship. The event was founded in 1974 and currently has the highest prize fund of any tournament in golf at roughly $12.5 million.

2. True. The WGC Match Play is one of the four annual World Golf Championships. Since 2016, it has been played at Austin Country Club in Texas.

3. A – Three. This is part of the Tour making an effort to have the FedEx Cup end before football season begins. Prior to 2019, the FedEx Cup Champion was decided in the middle of football season, which was hurting ratings.

4. B – Waste Management Open. It is hosted by TPC Scottsdale in Scottsdale, Arizona, typically in late January or early February. The most popular hole is the par-3 sixteenth where there is stadium seating surrounding it. Fans get there as early as 6 a.m. to get the best spots.

WHITE TEES

5. D – Florida. It is played at the Bay Hill Club and Lodge in Orlando, a private golf resort owned since 1974 by Palmer.

6. B – RBC Heritage. This tournament is played at Harbour Town Golf Links in Hilton Head, South Carolina.

7. B – Travelers Championship. It was originally founded in 1952 as the Insurance City Open. The title sponsors have changed multiple times, but it has been held at TPC River Highlands since 1984.

8. A – John Deere Classic. Hosted by TPC Deere Run in the Quad Cities community of Silvis, Illinois, usually there are always several charter planes going immediately to the site of the British Open following the tournament.

9. B – January. Currently, there is the Sentry Tournament of Champions at the Plantation Course in Kapalua and the Sony Open at the Waialae Country Club in Honolulu.

10. A – Bill Haas. Haas won the FedEx Cup in 2011. He defeated Hunter Mahan in a sudden death playoff at the third extra hole to win the TOUR Championship, which also allowed him to win the Cup.

11. C – Memorial Tournament. Founded in 1976, the tournament is played at Muirfield Village Golf Club in Dublin, Ohio, which is close to where Nicklaus grew up.

12. A – California. Since 1968, the event has been played at both courses at Torrey Pines in San Diego. Players play the North and South course on Thursday and Friday and then exclusively the South course over the weekend.

13. B – Justin Thomas. Thomas won seven tournaments over these two years.

14. False. Duval won the money title in 1998 where he won four tournaments.

15. True. These tournaments typically are in January and February and feature some of the best courses the Tour plays all year.

16. B – Only PGA Tour tournament winners from the previous year get invites. Since 1999, it has been played at the Plantation Course, which is a par 73, unlike most PGA Tour courses.

17. True. If a tournament can only complete 54 holes, full prize money and Fed Ex Cup are still awarded.

18. D – Florida. The PGA Tour headquarters are in Ponte Vedra Beach.

19. A – The Honda Classic. Holes 15–17 are three of the hardest holes on the entire PGA Tour. "I don't care if they make golf balls that go for a thousand yards. The Bear Trap will stand the test no matter what the equipment is," Jack Nicklaus once said.

20. B – Zurich Classic of New Orleans. In 2017, it became a team event. Alternate shot is played in Rounds 1 and 3 and then best ball is played in Rounds 2 and 4.

21. B – Texas. Following being renovated in 2015, Austin Country Club has hosted the event since 2016.

22. True. The British Open is considered an official PGA Tour tournament.

23. False. There is one PGA Tour event in Canada, the RBC Canadian Open, which is typically played in June.

24. B – A tour card for at least two years. While winning most tournaments gets you an invitation to the Masters, that is not the case for all of them.

25. True. This is why the tournament is called "the fifth major," and the players treat the week like it is.

26. B – Texas. Nelson, the tournament's first winner in 1944, was raised in the Fort Worth, Texas, area.

27. True. The ZoZo Championship was played in Japan for the first time in 2019 and Tiger Woods was the winner. The Tour played two other official events in Asia during a three-week period.

28. B – They offer comparable prize money to majors. The World Golf Championships are considered right below majors and the FedEx Cup in terms of importance for players on Tour.

29. A – Tiger Woods. Woods has won 18 overall, which is more than double any other player.

BLACK TEES

30. C – 2007. Tiger Woods was the first ever winner.

31. A – Tim Finchem. Finchem was the commissioner from 1994–2016. He also served in the White House during the administration of President Jimmy Carter.

32. B – 2013. The 2014 season technically began in October of 2013, as the Tour now applies a wrap-around season structure.

33. A – Joe Dey. Dey began his duties in 1969 and agreed to a five-year contract.

34. D – 3. Singh was the PGA Tour's leading money winner in 2003, 2004, and 2008.

35. B – Riviera Golf Club. This tournament has been played at Riviera on a near-continuous basis since 1973.

36. True. Both players have done extremely well at Pebble Beach. O'Meara's wins came in 1985, 1989, 1990, 1992, and 1997, while Mickelson's have come in 1998, 2005, 2007, 2012, and 2019.

37. D – 6. PGA Tour, PGA Tour Champions, Korn Ferry Tour, PGA Tour Latinoamérica, PGA Tour China, and PGA Tour Canada.

38. C – Travelers Championship. The other three tournaments have slightly smaller fields and do not follow the normal PGA Tour exemption categories, but the Travelers Championship has a normal field and follows normal PGA Tour exemption categories.

39. A – 1944. This event is one of the longest running tournaments on Tour.

40. D – 2019. Rookie Matthew Wolff won his first PGA Tour tournament at this event, which was held at TPC Twin Cities in Blaine, Minnesota.

XIV. PGA TOUR CHAMPIONS

QUESTIONS

Golf is a game that can be played regardless of age, which is why it only makes sense that there is a professional tour for older players. It follows a similar structure to the PGA Tour with majors and a season-long point system, but also has its differences.

Some players continue their success from the PGA Tour on the senior circuit, while others better their careers with stronger performances after graduating from the regular tour.

Some of the best players on the PGA Tour Champions (formerly Senior PGA Tour, Champions Tour) have included Bruce Fleisher, Hale Irwin, and most recently Bernhard Langer.

"I just never subscribed to the theory that at age 55, you fall off the face of the earth on the Tour. I always felt that was too young of an age for that."

–Hale Irwin

"There are far more important things in life than making a putt or missing a putt or winning a championship or losing a championship."

–Bernhard Langer

Answers for this section are on pages 189–191.

RED TEES

1. How many rounds are played in most events?
A. 2
B. 3
C. 4
D. 5

2. Who has dominated the PGA Tour Champions since his first money title in 2008?
A. Bernhard Langer
B. Tom Lehman
C. Davis Love III
D. Tom Watson

3. True/False: Like the PGA Tour, PGA Tour Champions has four majors.

WHITE TEES

4. What year was the PGA Tour Champions founded?
A. 1970
B. 1975
C. 1980
D. 1985

5. What is the minimum age to play in a PGA Tour Champions event?
A. 40
B. 45
C. 50
D. 55

6. Who took home the first PGA Tour Champions Rookie of the Year in 1990?
   A. Hale Irvin
   B. Dave Stockton
   C. Lee Trevino
   D. Jim Colbert

7. What is the PGA Tour Champions' equivalent to the PGA Tour's FedEx Cup?
   A. Wells Fargo Cup
   B. Charles Schwab Cup
   C. Fidelity Cup
   D. Walmart Cup

8. True/False: Recently, the PGA Tour Champions has had three straight majors in the month of July.

9. Which was not an official PGA Tour Champions tournament in 2019?
   A. Bass Pro Shops Legends of Golf
   B. Boeing Classic
   C. JetBlue Open
   D. Dick's Sporting Goods Open

10. Who holds the record for the biggest winning margin on the PGA Tour Champions (13 strokes)?
    A. Jack Nicklaus
    B. Bernhard Langer
    C. Lee Trevino
    D. Kevin Sutherland

11. True/False: The longest drive recorded on the PGA Tour Champions is 422 yards.

12. In what year did Vijay Singh win his first PGA Tour Champions major?
    A. 2012
    B. 2014
    C. 2016
    D. 2018

13. True/False: Fred Couples has never won a PGA Tour Champions major.

14. In what year did the Senior British Open become a major?
    A. 1985
    B. 1993
    C. 2003
    D. 2010

15. True/False: Generally, there are no cuts on the PGA Tour Champions.

BLACK TEES

16. True/False: The PGA Tour Champions has an award at the end named after Byron Nelson for the player who has the lowest scoring average.

17. In what year did Retief Goosen win his first PGA Tour Champions event?
    A. 2014
    B. 2015
    C. 2017
    D. 2019

18. Who holds the PGA Tour Champions record for most strokes under par (27-under) at a given tournament?

A. Bernhard Langer

B. Tom Lehman

C. Jack Nicklaus

D. Bruce Fleisher

19. As of 2019, how many 59s have been had on the PGA Tour Champions?

A. 0

B. 1

C. 10

D. 13

20. Who led the PGA Tour Champions in wins during the 1997 season with nine?

A. Hale Irwin

B. Dave Stockton

C. Jim Colbert

D. Tom Watson

XIV. PGA TOUR CHAMPIONS

ANSWERS

RED TEES

1. B – 3. Unlike the PGA Tour, these tournaments are contested over three days, typically Friday–Sunday.

2. A – Bernhard Langer. From 2008–18, Langer won ten of a possible eleven money titles.

3. False. PGA Tour Champions has five majors—The Tradition, Senior PGA Championship, U.S. Senior Open, Senior Players Championship, and The Senior Open Championship.

WHITE TEES

4. C – 1980. It was originally called the Senior PGA Tour.

5. C – 50. The Tour is open to players who are 50 years or older.

6. C – Lee Trevino. Not only did he win Rookie of the Year, he was also the Player of the Year and the leading money winner.

7. B – Charles Schwab Cup. It concludes with the Charles Schwab Cup Championship, which is typically played in November.

8. True. Between the end of June and July, the U.S. Senior Open, the Senior Players Championship, and the Senior Open Championship are held on consecutive weeks.

9. C – JetBlue Open. JetBlue is not currently a sponsor of the PGA Tour Champions.

10. B – Bernhard Langer. Langer won the 2014 Senior Open Championship by 13 strokes.

11. True. In 1996 at The Tradition, Jim Dent and Jay Sigel both recorded 422-yard drives.

12. D – 2018. His first PGA Tour Champions win came in 2017, but his first major was the 2018 Senior Players Championship.

13. False. Couples won the Senior Players Championship in 2011 and the Senior Open Championship in 2012.

14. C – 2003. Tom Watson was the winner. It was an official tournament since 1987, but not counted as a major on the PGA Tour Champions until 2003.

15. True. Since tournaments are typically three rounds and there are smaller fields (roughly 80 players), there are no cuts.

BLACK TEES

16. True. This award has been won almost exclusively by Bernhard Langer of late.

17. D – 2019. In his first year eligible, Goosen won the Senior Players Championship.

18. C – Jack Nicklaus. Nicklaus finished 27-under par at the 1990 Senior Players Championship.

19. B – 1. Kevin Sutherland is the only player to shoot a 59, which occurred in the second round of the 2014 Dick's Sporting Goods Open.

20. A – Hale Irwin. To no one's surprise, Irwin won Player of the Year and was the Tour's leading money winner that year as well.

XV. LPGA TOUR

QUESTIONS

While there are "LPGA Tours" around the world, the United States' was the first, most well-known and features the most elite players competing every week.

Like the men's tours, its popularity has grown over the years and now features total prize money in the $70 million range for the year. It also is shown almost every week on television, which only increases the exposure to fans around the world.

The Tour is most known for popular players such as Annika Sörenstam, Lorena Ochoa, Nancy Lopez, and Kathy Whitworth.

"I still get butterflies on the first tee. I still get sweaty hands, and my heart pumps a lot going down the 18th. But I know what winning is all about now, and that's a feeling that I like."

–Annika Sörenstam

"Doubt yourself and you doubt everything you see. Judge yourself and you see judges everywhere. But if you listen to the sound of your own voice, you can rise above doubt and judgment. And you can see forever."

–Nancy Lopez

Answers for this section are on pages 201–203.

RED TEES

1. True/False: The LPGA Tour has five major championships.

2. Which Swedish golfer, who retired in 2008 with 90 international titles, is widely regarded as the best female player ever?
   A. Nancy Lopez
   B. Annika Sörenstam
   C. Juli Inkster
   D. Helen Alfredsson

3. What is the LGPA equivalent to the Ryder Cup?
   A. Walker Cup
   B. President's Cup
   C. Solheim Cup
   D. None

WHITE TEES

4. Which LPGA golfer won nine tournaments in 1978, her rookie season?
   A. Helen Alfredsson
   B. Annika Sörenstam
   C. Nancy Lopez
   D. Judy Rankin

5. Who was the first International player to win the Rolex Player of the Year Award?
   A. Ayako Okamoto
   B. Laura Davies
   C. Se-ri Pak
   D. Annika Sörenstam

6. Who was the first LPGA player to shoot 59?
A. Meg Mallon
B. Nancy Lopez
C. Annika Sörenstam
D. Karrie Webb

7. In what year did Annika Sörenstam step away from the LPGA Tour to focus on business and family?
A. 2005
B. 2008
C. 2010
D. 2015

8. From 1994–2018 there was only one player from the United States to be the leading money winner. Who was it?
A. Stacy Lewis
B. Morgan Pressel
C. Lexi Thompson
D. Pat Bradley

9. From 1995–2005, Annika Sörenstam won eight money list titles. Who was the only other player to win during this time?
A. Lorena Ochoa
B. Karrie Webb
C. Beth Daniel
D. Se-ri Pak

10. Who has the most LPGA Tour titles with 88?
A. Kathy Whitworth
B. Annika Sörenstam
C. Nancy Lopez
D. Pat Bradley

11. Who is the youngest player ever to qualify to play in the U.S. Women's Open at age 12?
    A. Morgan Pressel
    B. Michelle Wei
    C. Lexi Thompson
    D. Paula Creamer

12. True/False: Michelle Wei has won one major championship.

13. Who was the first player to earn more than $1 million in a season?
    A. Annika Sörenstam
    B. Michelle Wei
    C. Nancy Lopez
    D. Karrie Webb

14. Who was the first golfer to win Rookie of the Year and Player of the Year in the same season?
    A. Nancy Lopez
    B. Lorena Ochoa
    C. Karrie Webb
    D. Pat Bradley

15. True/False: The first U.S. Women's Open was held in 1956.

16. What is the LPGA's equivalent of the Korn Ferry Tour?
    A. Web.com Tour
    B. Symetra Tour
    C. IMG Tour
    D. Charles Schwab Tour

17. What country is Juli Inkster from?
   A. England
   B. United States
   C. Canada
   D. Scotland

18. After which major is it a tradition to jump into the water next to the 18th green?
   A. U.S. Women's Open
   B. ANA Inspiration
   C. The Evian Championship
   D. Women's PGA Championship

19. In what year did the British Women's Open become a major?
   A. 1995
   B. 2001
   C. 2005
   D. 2010

20. True/False: Annika Sörenstam won three straight Women's PGA Championships in the 2000s.

BLACK TEES

21. In what year was the Women's British Open first played at the Old Course at St. Andrews?
   A. 1980
   B. 1997
   C. 2000
   D. 2007

22. In 2007, which player became the youngest player ever to win an LPGA major (18 years old) at the Kraft Nabisco?
    A. Se-ri Pak
    B. Morgan Pressel
    C. Inbee Park
    D. Jiyai Shin

23. How old was Michelle Wei when she turned professional?
    A. 16
    B. 18
    C. 20
    D. 22

24. True/False: In order to be inducted into the LPGA Hall of Fame a player must have played on tour for at least 10 seasons.

25. Who is the only player ever to win the LPGA Player of the Year, Rookie of the Year, and the Vare Trophy in the same year?
    A. Annika Sörenstam
    B. Lorena Ochoa
    C. Nancy Lopez
    D. Karrie Webb

26. True/False: The LPGA Tour has never had more than 30 tournaments in a season.

27. True/False: The LPGA Tour does not have a team tournament where two players compete together.

28. Annika Sörenstam's first LPGA Tour win came at what event in 1995?
    A. GHP Heartland Classic
    B. U.S. Women's Open
    C. Michelob Light Classic
    D. ShopRite LPGA Classic

29. In what year did Nancy Lopez win her final LPGA Tour event?
   A. 1990
   B. 1995
   C. 1997
   D. 2004

30. True/False: There has never been a year where an American has not won at least one major.

XV. LPGA TOUR

ANSWERS

RED TEES

1. True. The majors are: ANA Inspiration, U.S. Women's Open, Women's PGA Championship, Women's British Open, and the Evian Championship.

2. B – Annika Sörenstam. There's no question she was the best female player to ever play the game and had a huge impact on the sport.

3. C – Solheim Cup. The event was founded in 1990 and follows the same format as the Ryder Cup.

WHITE TEES

4. C – Nancy Lopez. Lopez went on to win 48 total LPGA Tour events, including three majors.

5. A – Ayako Okamoto. Okamoto won the award in 1987 where she won four tournaments, as well as finishing in the top-10 seventeen times.

6. C – Annika Sörenstam. The feat was accomplished in the second round of the Standard Register Ping in Phoenix in 2001.

7. B – 2008. Her last professional tournament was the Dubai Ladies Masters on the Ladies European Tour in December 2008 where she finished in seventh place.

8. A – Stacy Lewis. Lewis was the leading money winner in 2014 when she won three total tournaments.

9. B – Karrie Webb. Webb was the leading money winner in 1996, 1999, and 2000.

10. A – Kathy Whitworth. Whitworth was a fixture on the Tour with her wins coming from 1962–95.

11. C – Lexi Thompson. She played in the 2012 edition where she shot 86–82 and failed to make the cut.

12. True. Wei's lone major was the 2014 U.S. Women's Open.

13. D – Karrie Webb. This happened in 1996 when she won four tournaments, including one in her second-ever LPGA start.

14. A – Nancy Lopez. In 1978, Lopez won both awards.

15. False. It was first held in 1946 at Spokane Country Club where Patty Berg was the winner.

16. B – Symetra Tour. Although it has had different sponsor names over the years, it was originally founded in 1999.

17. B – United States. Inkster has won 31 times on the LPGA Tour.

18. B – ANA Inspiration. This has been a tradition since 1988 where players and their caddies jump into the water that is called "Champions Lake" or "Poppie's Pond."

19. B – 2001. While it was an official event for many years earlier, it was not an LPGA major until 2001.

20. True. Sörenstam won the event in 2003, 2004, and 2005. She won in a playoff and then by three strokes and five strokes.

BLACK TEES

21. D – 2007. It was won by Lorena Ochoa with a final score of 5-under par. She won by four strokes.

22. B – Morgan Pressel. Pressel won the event by one stroke over three players.

23. A – 16. In 1999 she officially turned pro and signed deals with Nike and Sony.

24. True. In addition, players must have done one of the following: win an LPGA major, the Vare Trophy, or Rolex Player of the Year.

25. C – Nancy Lopez. It was a clean sweep for Lopez in 1978.

26. False. Since 2014, the LPGA Tour has had more than 30 tournaments every season.

27. False. The Dow Great Lakes Bay Invitational is a team event.

28. B – U.S. Women's Open. Sörenstam defeated Meg Mallon by one stroke.

29. C – 1997. It occurred at the Chick-fil-A Charity Championship.

30. False. This has happened multiple times, including in 2012 and 2019.

XVI. RULES AND GOLF LANGUAGE

QUESTIONS

There's no question golf is a complicated game with many rules to learn and specific etiquette to abide by out on the course. There are a lot of golf purists out there who want the game played a certain way.

The game of golf is also special in the sense that the same rules apply to the PGA Tour as four buddies playing a casual weekend round together.

By and large, the majority of the rules are enforced by the USGA and the governing body is constantly tweaking them for the better of the game.

"Golf is a puzzle without an answer. I've played the game for 50 years and I still haven't the slightest idea of how to play."

—Gary Player

"Golf is the closest game to the game we call life. You get bad breaks from good shots; you get good breaks from bad shots—but you have to play the ball where it lies."

—Bobby Jones

Answers for this section are on pages 213–216.

RED TEES

1. Going by proper golf etiquette, who should tee off first on the second tee?
   A. Player who had the highest score on hole one
   B. Player who had the lowest score on hole one
   C. Player who putted last on hole one
   D. Player listed second on scorecard

2. When dropping a golf ball, where should a player's hand be?
   A. Shoulder height
   B. Knee height
   C. Ground level
   D. Waist height

3. What is it called when you hit a second shot because you believe your first shot may be lost?
   A. Mulligan
   B. Gimme
   C. Provisional
   D. Re-do

4. What is it called when a player records an eight on a hole?
   A. Snowman
   B. Crazy eight
   C. Double-four
   D. Double bogey

5. What is the ranger's job at a golf course?
   A. Pick up balls at driving range
   B. Make sure animals stay off course
   C. Make sure players are keeping up with pace of play
   D. Check players in at pro shop

6. When a right-hander says he/she hits a draw, what direction does the ball go?
   A. Left-to-right
   B. Right-to-left
   C. Dead straight
   D. Low-to-high

7. What is proper etiquette when a player gets a hole-in-one?
   A. Everyone buys him/her drinks
   B. He/she buys everyone drinks
   C. Each player in group gives $100
   D. He/she gets free round

WHITE TEES

8. What's the maximum number of clubs allowed in a player's golf bag during a round?
   A. 14
   B. 18
   C. 10
   D. 16

9. How many rounds must a golfer play to be eligible for a USGA handicap?
   A. 1
   B. 5
   C. 10
   D. 29

10. What constitutes a free drop?
   A. Water hazard
   B. Ground under repair
   C. Lateral hazard
   D. Out of bounds

11. True/False: If a player hits a ball off of the tee without the intent to hit the ball, he/she is allowed to replace the ball on the tee without a penalty.

12. On which shot does the flagstick need to come out before the ball goes into the hole?
    A. Bunker shot
    B. Putt from green
    C. Putt from fringe
    D. None, it can stay in at all times

13. Under USGA rules, how long are you permitted to search for a lost ball?
    A. 5 minutes
    B. 10 minutes
    C. 3 minutes
    D. Until group behind you reaches tee box

14. True/False: The edge of a penalty area should be defined by stakes, lines or physical features.

15. True/False: When a player putts a ball on the fringe it is not considered an official putt.

16. True/False: In stroke play, after a hole is completed, a player may hit a putt again with no penalty.

17. True/False: When a player putts the ball close to the hole, they have the option of finishing no matter where the other balls on the green are.

18. Women's tees at courses are typically which color?
A. Black
B. Purple
C. Red
D. Green

19. True/False: There is a two-stroke penalty for stepping in someone's line on the putting green.

20. What is the format called a scramble?
A. Each player plays their own ball and the best score out of the group is recorded
B. Each player hits a shot, the best one is selected and each player then plays from there until the ball is in the hole
C. Each player plays their own ball until the green and then only one player putts
D. Each hole has a different player who has their score count. Every player needs to have their score count at least once.

21. True/False: Shots can never be hit off the cart path.

22. True/False: If a ball lands in a divot in the fairway, the player still must play it as it lies.

23. What do white stakes indicate?
A. Penalty area
B. Out of bounds
C. Water hazard
D. Don't drive carts beyond that point

24. A player hits a ball into a pond in front of the tee on a par-3. What can't he/she do?
    A. Drop on other side
    B. Re-tee
    C. Go to drop zone
    D. Drop two club lengths from where it entered

BLACK TEES

25. What is the penalty for a double-hit on the same swing?
    A. None
    B. Two strokes
    C. Replay shot
    D. One stroke

26. In match play, after the hole has begun, the players agree to consider the hole tied. What is the ruling?
    A. Replay the entire match
    B. Replay that hole
    C. Both players get disqualified
    D. No penalty

27. True/False: In match play, both players must agree to stop play in event of bad weather.

28. What is the slope of a golf course?
    A. How hilly it is
    B. Tells bogey golfers how difficult it will be
    C. What a scratch golfer would shoot over two rounds
    D. How long it will take to play

29. How far behind the tee markers are players allowed to tee off from?

    A. 5 feet

    B. 2 club lengths

    C. A driver length

    D. Unlimited

30. What is an albatross?

    A. Double-eagle (three-under par)

    B. Triple-bogey (three-over par)

    C. Holing out from fairway on par-4

    D. Double par

XVI. RULES AND GOLF LANGUAGE

ANSWERS

RED TEES

1. B – Player who had the lowest score on hole 1. Golf etiquette says the order on the tee should be from lowest score to highest score from the previous hole.

2. B – Knee height. This was a recent change as before it was shoulder height, but it was adjusted to make it fairer for everyone. Some thought shorter players had an advantage with dropping balls from shoulder height.

3. C – Provisional. If you hit a provisional and find your original shot, you must play that ball. But, if you don't then you play the provisional and take whatever penalty strokes that need to be taken.

4. A – Snowman. This is an old saying that goes back years. It doesn't matter whether it's a par-3 or par-5, an eight is still a snowman.

5. C – Make sure players are keeping up with pace of play. If a group is slow and keeping other groups waiting, typically the ranger will tell them to pick up the pace. They usually drive around on a golf cart with a flag to signal they are the ranger.

6. B – Right-to-left. A player has a fade when the ball goes left-to-right.

7. B – He/she buys everyone drinks. While some would say it should be the other way around, proper etiquette has the player who records the ace buying drinks for everyone.

WHITE TEES

8. A – 14. Players can use whatever clubs they want, but the number cannot exceed 14.

9. C – 10. Once players get a lot of scores, the best 10 from the previous 20 are taken, but to start a player only needs 10.

10. B – Ground under repair. Usually, courses have these areas marked with a painted circle. This could be anything from drainage ditches to areas of grass that are being re-sodded.

11. True. As long as the player did not intend to hit it, he/she can replace it without penalty. That goes for anywhere on the course, too.

12. D – None, it can stay in at all times. This was another rule change where players do not get penalized for holing out a shot with the pin still in the hole.

13. C – 3 minutes. The previous rule of five minutes has been changed to three minutes to help with pace of play.

14. True. Players need to know where penalty areas are on a course.

15. True. An official putt is only when the ball is on the green.

16. False. In match play, players can hit putts again without penalty, but not stroke play.

17. True. Proper etiquette allows players to finish out the hole permitting they do not step in anyone else's line.

18. C – Red. Some courses use a different color system, but generally red tees are reserved for the women.

19. False. While it is frowned upon, there is no penalty.

20. B – Each player hits a shot, the best one is selected and each player then plays from there until the ball is in the hole. This format is used the most at golf outings.

21. False. While more often than not players use the relief they can get, there's no rule that says players cannot hit off cart paths.

22. True. Unless playing with a local rule of rolling the ball over in your own fairway, this shot must be played how it lies. This comes into play sometimes on the PGA Tour.

23. B – Out of bounds. Usually this is the golf course's property line. Any balls outside of it are considered out of bounds.

24. A – Drop on the other side. That would be an illegal drop.

BLACK TEES

25. A – None. It used to be a one-stroke penalty, but a recent rule change no longer has it being a penalty.

26. D – No penalty. In match play, as long as the two players agree on something, it is fair game.

27. False. If one player says he/she doesn't want to play on, the match is stopped.

28. B – Tells bogey golfers how difficult it will be. Along with a course rating, the slope is found on almost every scorecard.

29. B – 2 club lengths. It can be any clubs, too.

30. A – Double-eagle (three-under par). There have been 18 albatrosses recorded in major tournament history.

AFTERWORD

It was a Tuesday afternoon and I had a big decision to make—Do I travel from my home in Orlando, Florida, to Quintana Roo, Mexico, and hope I get into the PGA Tour's Maykoba Golf Classic at the last minute?

I was the eighth alternate on Friday and then the weekend went by and come Monday morning I was the fourth alternate. Then came Tuesday when I was alerted by the Tour that I was now the first alternate.

If I went, I would be risking potentially traveling all the way there for nothing, which would include paying for flights, lodging, and food. But, as a professional golfer since 2002, playing on all of the mini-Tours for many years before securing a PGA Tour card for the first time in 2016, getting the chance to play in a PGA Tour event isn't something that should be taken for granted.

These scenarios play out each and every week—they just aren't heavily featured publicly. Most people just know professional golf from what happens Sunday afternoons when players cash in huge checks for their week's work, but it's far from reality.

So, Wednesday afternoon I hopped on a JetBlue flight and got to the tournament site late at night with the first round scheduled to begin in a few hours. There had been quite a bit of rain early in the week and thunderstorms were forecasted for Thursday and Friday, the first two days of the event.

Thursday morning, my gamble paid off as Jason Dufner withdrew from the event, and I was the last player in the field.

The first round was eventually cancelled Thursday due to rain, which meant more time for me to get settled. It also meant finding more lodging accommodations since the first and second rounds would be Friday and Saturday with the third and fourth rounds being played Sunday and into Monday.

Unfortunately, I missed the cut after the second round and flew back to Orlando after staying in three different hotels during my short stay.

It was a net financial loss for the week.

But, the gamble certainly was worth it as the rewards from a top-10 finish or even a victory would have been life-changing.

Life as a professional golfer isn't as glamorous and easy-going as it may seem for everyone. But, there's a lot of things that make it all worth it.

For myself, I have been to a ton of really cool places, met some great people, and had some incredible experiences along the way.

One of the best was in 2017 when I was paired with Bill Belichick in the AT&T Pebble Beach Pro-Am. I knew weeks in advance I would be partnered with the coach of my favorite professional team. They were going to be in the Super Bowl against the Falcons in Houston, so I had to go, right?

The Patriots completed the greatest comeback in Super Bowl history, defeating the Falcons in overtime after trailing 28–3 in the third quarter. And just a few days later, I was on the famed Pebble Beach golf course with Belichick, the greatest coach of all-time just days after he won the Super Bowl.

And what an experience it was. Not only did I get to golf four rounds with Belichick, I also had my best finish on Tour—a tie for eighth.

All the hours of practice, along with days on the road away from family, become worth it with weeks like that.

Approaching forty years old, in all other sports my time would be coming to an end, but not golf. This is something that makes the game so great. Some players reach their peaks in their forties, and there is a level playing field among all players. It doesn't matter if someone is forty-five or twenty-five.

Also, there are no five-year contracts like other sports; what you make is based on how you scored. It doesn't matter what it looks like or how you get it done. If you scored better than the competition that particular week you get rewarded for it.

Having success on Tour also isn't always about having the most skill. The off-course facet is equally important.

Golf isn't a team sport where there are others constantly surrounding you to build or pick you up, you are your own team and it is up to you to build your own team around you.

Most of that is at home with a family that is constantly providing encouragement along with support and making it as easy as possible to be on the road almost 75 percent of the year.

Certainly, the lifestyle isn't for everyone, but I wouldn't want it any other way.

The pages before this were focused heavily the game's greatest players and moments that deserve to be enjoyed, but just remember for every great player there's a story like mine and someone grinding every week to make a living.

–Rob Oppenheim